UZBEKISTAN

BAHRAIN

CYPRUS

IRAN

ISRAEL

JORDAN

KUWAIT

LEBANON

OMAN

QATAR

SAUDI ARABIA

SYRIA

TURKEY

UNITED ARAB EMIRATES

YEMEN

AFGHANISTAN

BANGLADESH

BHUTAN

INDIA

NEPAL

PAKISTAN

SRI LANKA

MALDIVES

CHINA

JAPAN

MONGOLIA

SOUTH KOREA

NORTH KOREA

TAIWAN

HONG KONG

BRUNEI

MYANMAR (BURMA)

CAMBODIA (KAMPUCHEA)

INDONESIA

LAOS

MALAYSIA

SINGAPORE

THAILAND

PHILIPPINES

VIETNAM

ALGERIA

BENIN

BURKINA FASO

CAMEROON

CAPE VERDE

CENTRAL AFRICAN REPUBLIC

CHAD

DJIBOUTI

EGYPT

PICTURE ATLAS

FOR CHILDREN

Illustrated by Nicholas Price

Text by Julia Gorton

Editors: Julia Gorton and Angela Royston
Editorial Assistants: Kim Kremer and Lakshmi Hughes
Designers: Maggie Aldred and Cathy Tincknell
Design Assistant: Julie Marston
Picture Researcher: Emily Hedges
Production Controller: Ruth Charlton

First published in Great Britain in 1994 by
George Philip Limited

This edition published in 1998 by Hamlyn Children's Books,
an imprint of Egmont Children's Books Limited,
Michelin House, 81 Fulham Road, London SW3 6RB

ISBN 0 600 59535 8

A CIP catalogue record for this book is available at the British Library

Printed in Italy

CONTENTS

WHAT IS A MAP?

From space, the Earth looks like a huge, round ball, covered mostly by water and partly by land. The shape of each piece of land and sea, and the names we give to them, can be shown on a map. Maps give a kind of picture of the Earth's surface, as if we were looking down from above. The detail shown on a map depends on how far above the surface the "picture" was taken.

If you were orbiting Earth in a satellite, you could look down and see the whole of Africa. But you would not be able to see much more detail, except for the highest mountains and the biggest lakes.

Shrinking to fit

▲ A map is a small picture of a big area, so everything it shows has to be shrunk to fit in. This diesel locomotive is really nearly 15 metres long, but here it's less than 30 millimetres. It has been scaled down, and the scale bar tells us by how much - 10 mm or 1 cm in the drawing represents 5 metres on the ground.

◀ Here, the scale bar shows that the picture covers a wider area, as if we were looking at the train from further away. Now, 1 cm on the drawing represents 50 metres on the ground, so the train looks much smaller.

▶ If you look down on the scene from above and from further away again, you can't see actual objects at all. Now we need to use labelled symbols, as on a true map.

Somewhere Town

Splashy Pond

Flat maps of the Earth, which show all the land and sea at once, are very useful. But it is not easy to make a flat map of a round object. Map-makers have special ways of doing this. Sometimes, they have to stretch and bend the land shapes to make them fit into the area they want, so the actual shapes shown are not quite as accurate as they are on a globe.

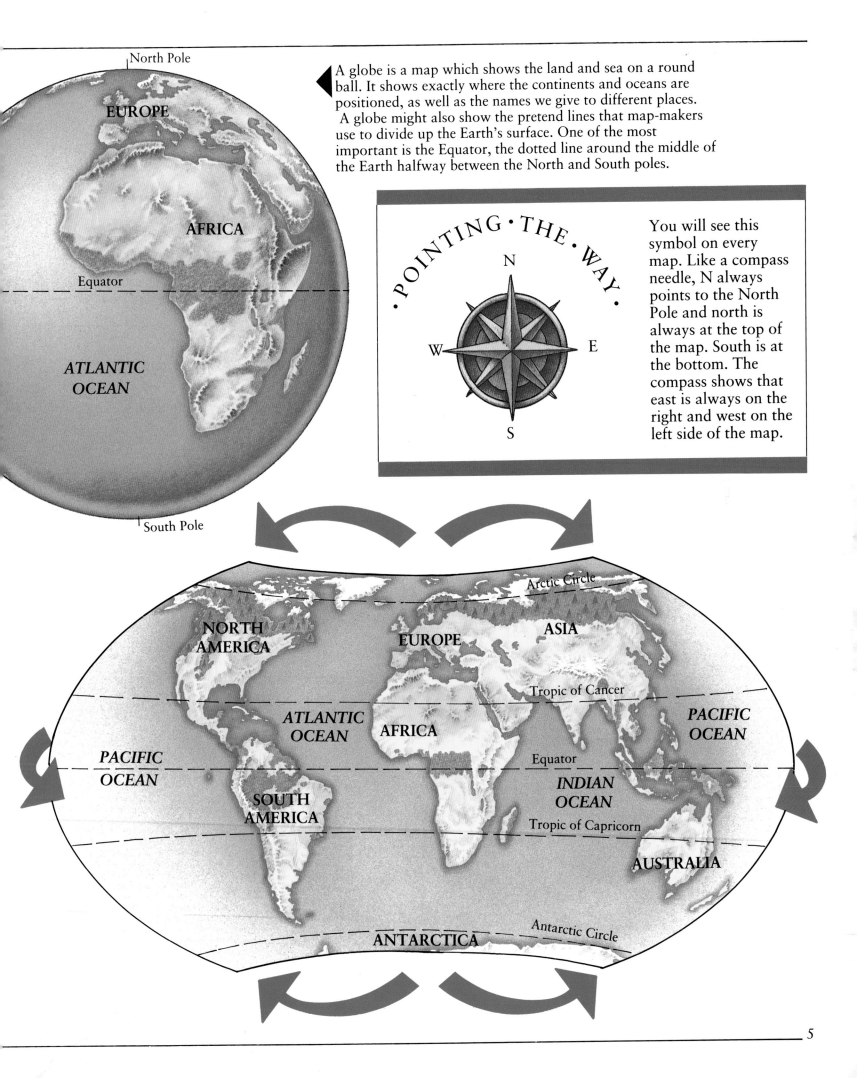

North Pole

EUROPE

AFRICA

Equator

ATLANTIC OCEAN

South Pole

A globe is a map which shows the land and sea on a round ball. It shows exactly where the continents and oceans are positioned, as well as the names we give to different places. A globe might also show the pretend lines that map-makers use to divide up the Earth's surface. One of the most important is the Equator, the dotted line around the middle of the Earth halfway between the North and South poles.

· POINTING · THE · WAY ·

N

W   E

S

You will see this symbol on every map. Like a compass needle, N always points to the North Pole and north is always at the top of the map. South is at the bottom. The compass shows that east is always on the right and west on the left side of the map.

Arctic Circle

NORTH AMERICA

EUROPE

ASIA

Tropic of Cancer

ATLANTIC OCEAN

AFRICA

PACIFIC OCEAN

PACIFIC OCEAN

Equator

INDIAN OCEAN

SOUTH AMERICA

Tropic of Capricorn

AUSTRALIA

Antarctic Circle

ANTARCTICA

HOT AND COLD PLACES

It is always hot around the Equator and cold at the North and South poles. Some parts of the Earth get plenty of rain, but some get hardly any rain at all. Different climates suit different kinds of plants and so produce different environments for animals and people to live in. The map opposite shows you the main environments in the world. Apart from the Countries of the World map, all the maps in this book use these colours to show the different environments.

Spreading the sunshine

Sunshine spreads thinly across the ground at the poles. It is always cold here, especially in winter.

The further you go from the Equator, the colder it gets. Countries between the tropics and the poles have warm summers and cold winters.

Arctic Circle

Tropic of Cancer

Equator

Sunshine is strongest in the tropics, between the lines on the map called the Tropic of Capricorn and the Tropic of Cancer. The climate here is always hot, with wet and dry seasons.

Tropic of Capricorn

Although there are thick forests at the foot of these mountains, no plants at all grow on their peaks. This is because the air gets colder and colder as you get higher up.

Very few plants or trees can survive in deserts like this because the blazing sun is too harsh and the sandy soil is too dry.

A forest of pine, spruce and other evergreen trees stretches as far as the eye can see. The huge evergreen forests in Canada and northern Asia and Europe are called the taiga. The taiga of northern Asia is the largest forest in the world.

It is so cold in the Arctic and Antarctic that even parts of the sea freeze over. Ice that floats on the surface of the sea is called pack ice. In the short polar summer, some of the pack ice melts, but it soon freezes again as the long, bitter winter sets in.

Icy places/ mountain ranges

Evergreen forest

Desert

Tropical rainforest

Woodland

Grassland and scrub

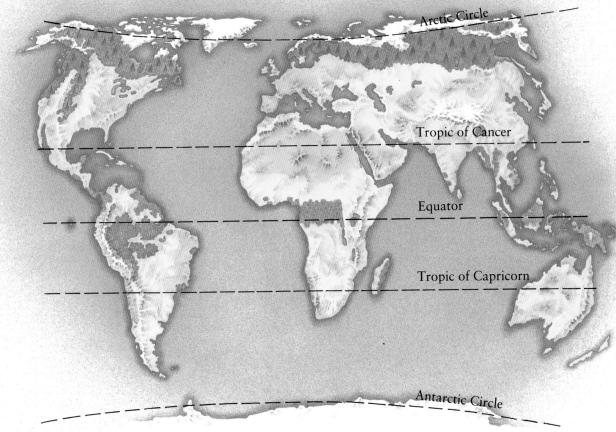

Arctic Circle

Tropic of Cancer

Equator

Tropic of Capricorn

Antarctic Circle

Plants grow so thickly in tropical rainforests that it is almost dark near the ground. The air here is hot and damp. Some rainforest trees can reach as high as 40 m or more. Twisting creepers grow up and around their trunks to get a share of the sunlight.

Natural grassland is too dry for many trees to grow, but it is good for grazing animals and farming crops.

7

LOOK CLOSER!

Maps try to show you as much as possible about the huge areas they represent, but they can only fit in the most important cities, and the biggest rivers, lakes and mountains. Look at the small pictures to find out more about each country. They tell you how the people live, what they eat, the kinds of things that they make, and what plants and animals are usually found there. The pictures are not, of course, drawn to match the size of the other things on the map. A whole city is shown just by a dot, but beside it you may see a picture of a single, famous building in that city.

All countries have farms. Some of the pictures on the maps show the kinds of crops that are grown, or the types of animals that are raised. Rice, one of the main food crops in China, is grown in special, flooded fields called paddy fields.

Red pandas, like this one, live in bamboo forests in the mountains of southwestern China. Look out for pictures of wild animals on all the maps. You'll see that the type of animal you find depends on both the landscape and the weather of each different area.

These children are wearing brightly-coloured, embroidered kimonos, the traditional dress of Japan. You'll find pictures of traditional dress on many of the maps. They show the kind of clothes that people in that area wear, sometimes for everyday use, but more often for special occasions.

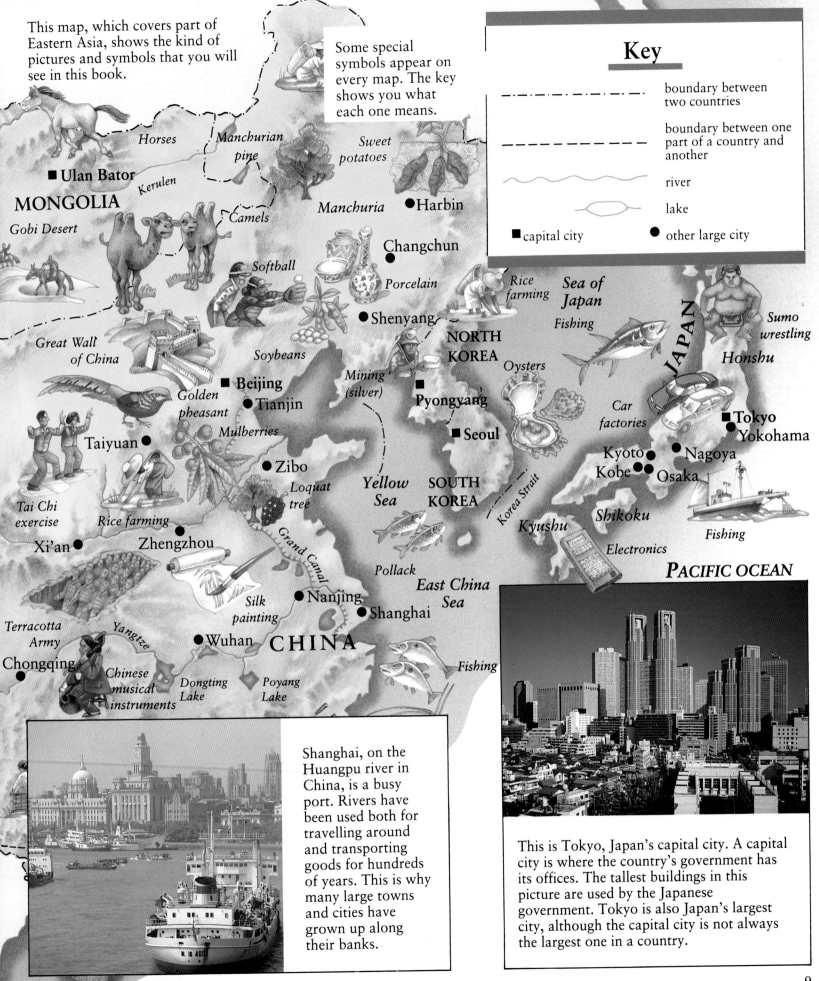

This map, which covers part of Eastern Asia, shows the kind of pictures and symbols that you will see in this book.

Some special symbols appear on every map. The key shows you what each one means.

Key

—··—··—	boundary between two countries
— — — —	boundary between one part of a country and another
～～～	river
⬭	lake
■ capital city	● other large city

Horses

Manchurian pine

Sweet potatoes

■ Ulan Bator

Kerulen

MONGOLIA

Gobi Desert

Camels

Manchuria

● Harbin

Softball

Porcelain

● Changchun

Rice farming

Sea of Japan

Fishing

JAPAN

Sumo wrestling

Honshu

Great Wall of China

Soybeans

Shenyang ●

NORTH KOREA

Oysters

Car factories

■ Beijing

Golden pheasant

Mining (silver)

■

● Tianjin

Pyongyang

■ Tokyo

Yokohama

Taiyuan ●

Mulberries

■ Seoul

Kyoto ● ● Nagoya

Kobe ●

● Osaka

● Zibo

Yellow Sea

SOUTH KOREA

Korea Strait

Loquat tree

Tai Chi exercise

Rice farming

Kyushu

Shikoku

Electronics

Xi'an ●

Zhengzhou ●

Grand Canal

Pollack

East China Sea

PACIFIC OCEAN

Silk painting

● Nanjing

Terracotta Army

Yangtze

● Wuhan

CHINA

Shanghai ●

Chongqing ●

Chinese musical instruments

Dongting Lake

Poyang Lake

Fishing

Fishing

Shanghai, on the Huangpu river in China, is a busy port. Rivers have been used both for travelling around and transporting goods for hundreds of years. This is why many large towns and cities have grown up along their banks.

This is Tokyo, Japan's capital city. A capital city is where the country's government has its offices. The tallest buildings in this picture are used by the Japanese government. Tokyo is also Japan's largest city, although the capital city is not always the largest one in a country.

COUNTRIES
OF THE WORLD

People have divided the continents into more than 170 different countries. Each one has its own government and flag. You can see all the flags at the beginning and end of the book. Some countries are so small they are shown on the map only by a number. Look at the list of numbers to find their names. Antarctica is not shown at all because no one lives there and no country rules it.

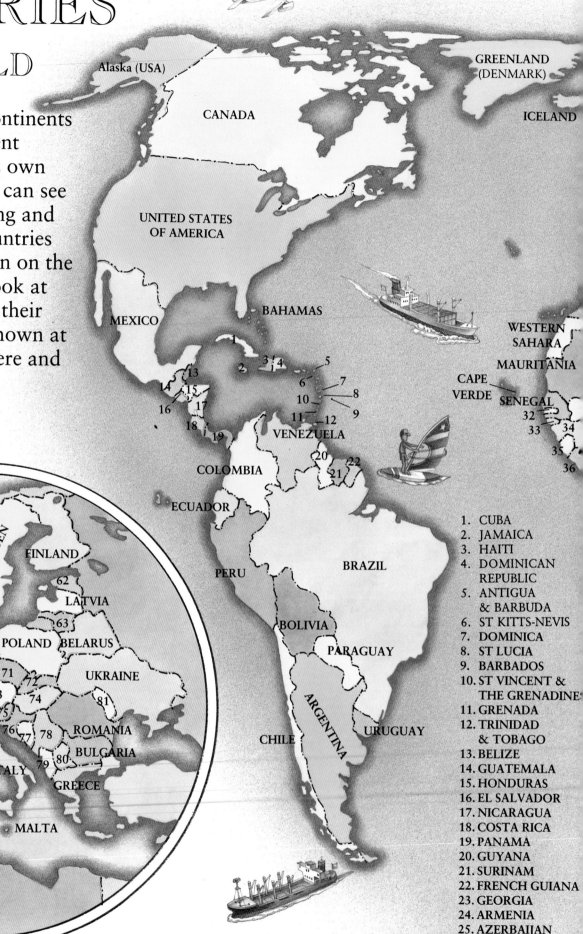

1. CUBA
2. JAMAICA
3. HAITI
4. DOMINICAN REPUBLIC
5. ANTIGUA & BARBUDA
6. ST KITTS-NEVIS
7. DOMINICA
8. ST LUCIA
9. BARBADOS
10. ST VINCENT & THE GRENADINE
11. GRENADA
12. TRINIDAD & TOBAGO
13. BELIZE
14. GUATEMALA
15. HONDURAS
16. EL SALVADOR
17. NICARAGUA
18. COSTA RICA
19. PANAMA
20. GUYANA
21. SURINAM
22. FRENCH GUIANA
23. GEORGIA
24. ARMENIA
25. AZERBAIJAN

The Pacific Ocean is too large to include on this map so these island groups are not shown:
Kiribati
Nauru
Tonga
Tuvalu
Western Samoa
Vanuatu
Fiji
Solomon Islands
Belau

This area is enlarged on the opposite page to make it easier to read.

RUSSIA

KAZAKHSTAN

MONGOLIA

NORTH KOREA

UZBEKISTAN

23
24 25
55

TURKEY

TURKMENISTAN

56

CHINA

SOUTH KOREA

JAPAN

MOROCCO

27 28

IRAQ

29
30 31

IRAN

AFGHANISTAN

26

ALGERIA

LIBYA

EGYPT

SAUDI ARABIA

31

52
53
54

PAKISTAN

NEPAL

57

58

INDIA

TAIWAN

OMAN

MYANMAR (BURMA)

59

PHILIPPINES

MALI

NIGER

CHAD

ERITREA

SUDAN

YEMEN

44

THAILAND

60

VIETNAM

38

NIGERIA

CAMEROON

CENTRAL AFRICAN REPUBLIC

ETHIOPIA

SOMALI REPUBLIC

SRI LANKA

BRUNEI

37

39
40 42

MALDIVES

MALAYSIA

43

GABON

CONGO

ZAIRE

45

46

KENYA

61

47

TANZANIA

SEYCHELLES

INDONESIA

PAPUA NEW GUINEA

ANGOLA

ZAMBIA

48

MOZAMBIQUE

NAMIBIA

ZIMBABWE

64. THE NETHERLANDS
65. BELGIUM
66. LUXEMBOURG
67. ANDORRA
68. SWITZERLAND
69. MONACO
70. LIECHTENSTEIN
71. THE CZECH REPUBLIC
72. SLOVAKIA
73. AUSTRIA
74. HUNGARY
75. SLOVENIA
76. CROATIA
77. BOSNIA-HERZEGOVINA
78. YUGOSLAVIA
79. ALBANIA
80. MACEDONIA
81. MOLDOVA
82. SAN MARINO
83. VATICAN CITY

BOTSWANA

49

MADAGASCAR

AUSTRALIA

50

SOUTH AFRICA

NEW ZEALAND

26. TUNISIA
27. CYPRUS
28. SYRIA
29. LEBANON
30. ISRAEL
31. JORDAN
32. GAMBIA
33. GUINEA-BISSAU
34. GUINEA
35. SIERRA LEONE
36. LIBERIA
37. IVORY COAST
38. BURKINA FASO
39. GHANA
40. TOGO
41. BENIN

42. SÃO TOMÉ & PRINCIPE
43. EQUATORIAL GUINEA
44. DJIBOUTI
45. UGANDA
46. RWANDA
47. BURUNDI
48. MALAWI
49. SWAZILAND
50. LESOTHO
51. KUWAIT
52. BAHRAIN

53. QATAR
54. UNITED ARAB EMIRATES
55. KYRGYZSTAN
56. TAJIKISTAN
57. BHUTAN
58. BANGLADESH
59. LAOS
60. CAMBODIA (KAMPUCHEA)
61. SINGAPORE
62. ESTONIA
63. LITHUANIA

WESTERN EUROPE

Most of Western Europe has mild weather, although the far north of Scotland can be bitterly cold in winter, whilst Italy and Spain have baking hot summers. There are no deserts in this part of the world. The eight major countries packed into this area all have a large number of towns and cities, lots of industry, and many roads, railways and airports to make travelling around easier.

The HIGHEST MOUNTAIN in Western Europe is Mont Blanc in France. It is 4,807 m high.

Over 20 MILLION Volkswagen "Beetle" cars have been made since production started in Germany in 1938.

Solero de Jerez is the FASTEST FLAMENCO DANCER on record. He can tap his heels 16 times per second.

The LONGEST ROAD TUNNEL in the world is the St Gotthard tunnel in Switzerland. It is 16.32 km long.

POLAND

Destruction of Berlin wall

Berlin

GERMANY

Dresden

THE CZECH REPUBLIC

Hogs

Stein of beer

Mercedes-Benz cars

Skiing

Hamburg

Frankfurters

Cologne Cathedral

Castles

Music

DENMARK

Bonn

Windmill

THE NETHERLANDS

Amsterdam

Rotterdam

Luxury chocolates

Brussels

BELGIUM

LX

Mining (iron ore)

Lille

Paris

Eiffel Tower

Seine

Apples

Cod

Cross-channel ferry

London

Houses of Parliament

Shakespeare

Cricket

Stonehenge

Dairy cattle

Cod

Oil and natural gas

NORTH SEA

Cod

Puffin

UNITED KINGDOM

Wedgewood china

Edinburgh castle

Edinburgh

Golf

Horse jumping

Rugby

Salmon

Ben Nevis

Glasgow

Scotch whisky

Tossing the caber

Belfast

IRELAND

Dublin

Horse racing

Salmon

Gannet

Giant's Causeway

Irish whiskey

Potatoes

Lobster

ATLANTIC OCEAN

N

E

W

S

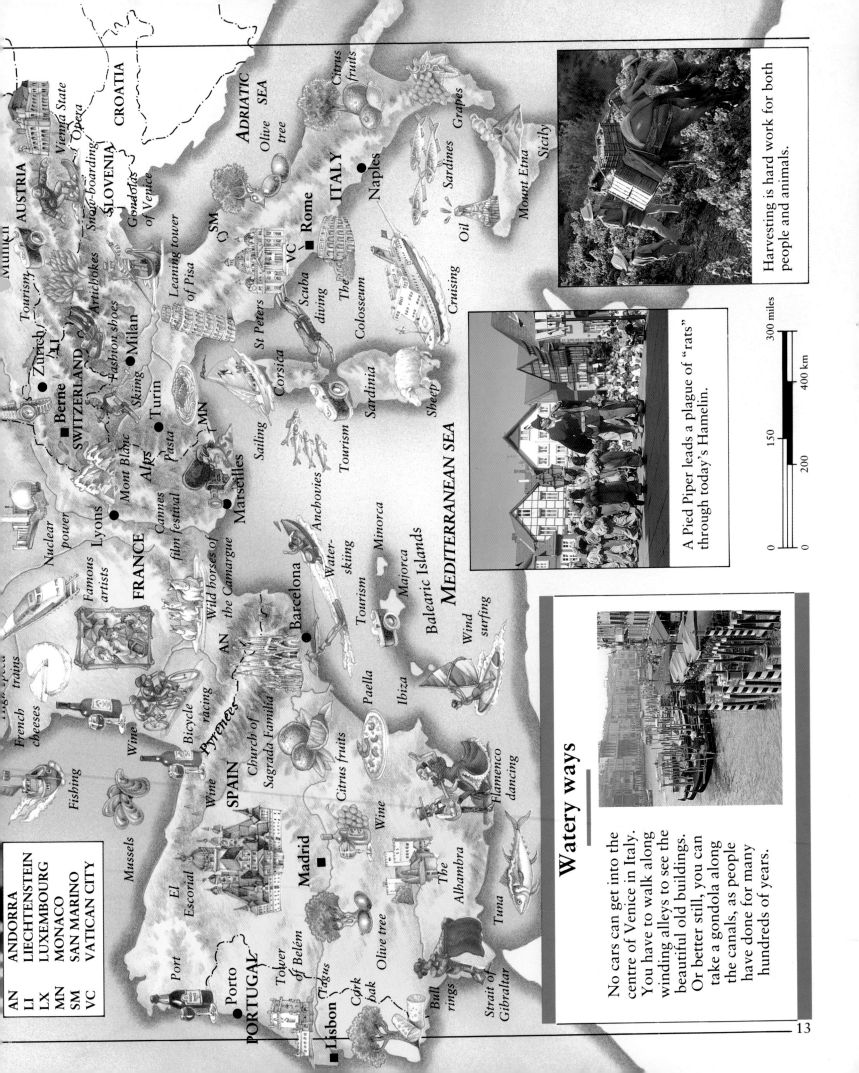

Harvesting is hard work for both people and animals.

A Pied Piper leads a plague of "rats" through today's Hamelin.

Watery ways

No cars can get into the centre of Venice in Italy. You have to walk along winding alleys to see the beautiful old buildings. Or better still, you can take a gondola along the canals, as people have done for many hundreds of years.

EASTERN EUROPE

Mountains cover most of East Europe except in Poland and Hungary. The river Danube flows through flat farm-land across Hungary and Yugoslavia and between Romania and Bulgaria. The winters are cold in the north and in the mountains. Summer is hot, especially in the south. Many tourists come to Greece to enjoy the sunshine.

Best dresses

Two Polish girls, dressed up for a special occasion. They are wearing the national costume for their region. Poland has many national costumes because many different groups of people live within its borders.

Baltic Sea

Sunbathing

Shipbuilding

Gdansk

Tourism

E

Striped field mouse

Flax

European bison

Birch tree

Wisła

Warsaw

POLAND

Łódź

Potatoes

Outdoor cafes

Wheat

UKRAINE

Pine forests

Prut

MOLDOVA

Carpathian Mountains

Bran Castle

Wolf

Slav

Wild boar

ROMANIA

Factories

Folk dancing

Kraków

Flower market

Skiing

Chamois goat

Tisza

Geese

European hamster

Pigs

Mining (copper)

Traditional farming

Pigs

N

W

E

S

GERMANY

Charles Bridge

Bohemian crystal

Prague

CZECH REPUBLIC

Beer

Factories

Skiing

Wooden houses

Walking and biking

Open-air Catholic service

Car factory

Bratislava

Church in Brno

AUSTRIA

Paddle steamer on Danube

SLOVAKIA

Wine

Slav wedding

Budapest

HUNGARY

Sailing on Lake Balaton

SLOVENIA

Ljubljana

Zagreb CROATIA

Sunflowers

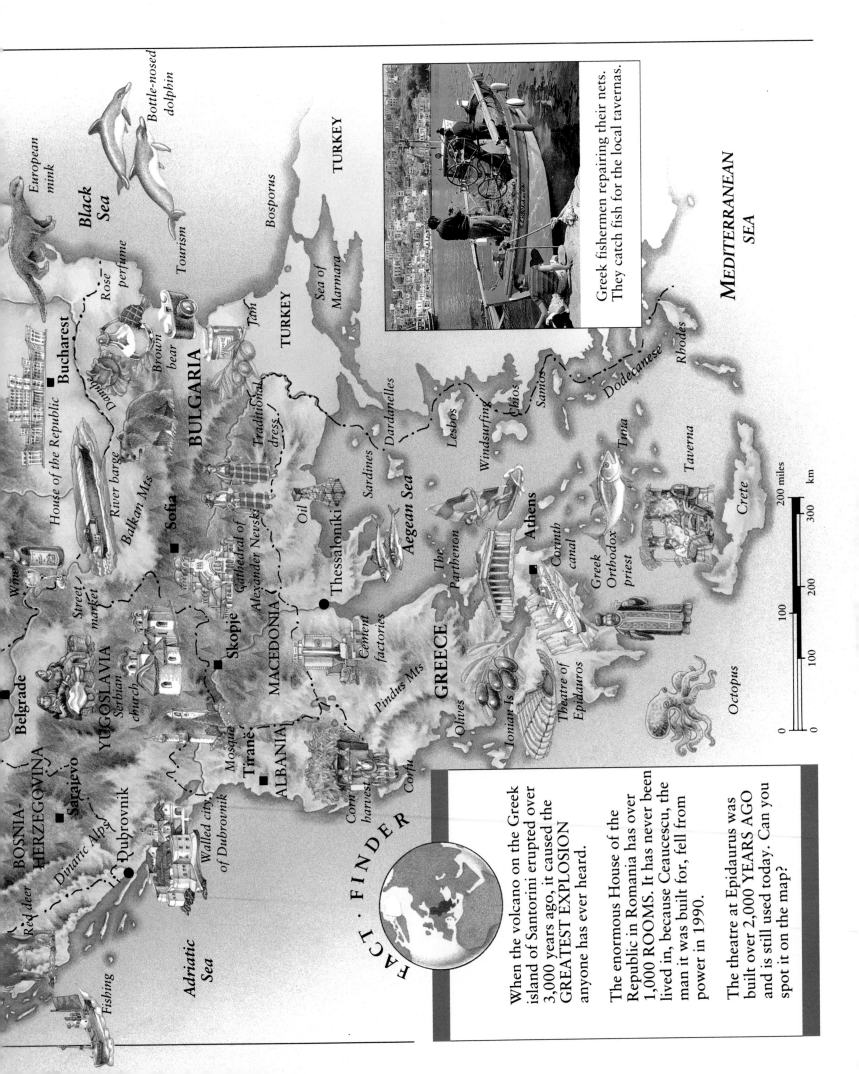

European mink

Bottle-nosed dolphin

Red deer

Black Sea

Rosé perfume

Bucharest

Brown bear

Tourism

House of the Republic

Danube

River barge

Balkan Mts

BULGARIA

Traditional dress

Tah

TURKEY

Bosporus

TURKEY

Sea of Marmara

Dardanelles

Sardines

Aegean Sea

Lesbos

Windsurfing

Chios

Samos

Dodecanese

Rhodes

Greek fishermen repairing their nets. They catch fish for the local tavernas.

Wine

Street market

Dinaric Alps

Belgrade

Sofia

Cathedral of Alexander Nevski

Oil

Thessaloniki

Cement factories

Pindus Mts

GREECE

Tuna

The Parthenon

Athens

Corinth canal

Greek Orthodox priest

Taverna

Crete

BOSNIA-HERZEGOVINA

Serbian church

YUGOSLAVIA

Sarajevo

Mosque

Skopje

MACEDONIA

Tiranë

ALBANIA

Walled city of Dubrovnik

Dubrovnik

Fishing

Adriatic Sea

Corn harvest

Corfu

Olives

Ionian Is.

Theatre of Epidauros

Octopus

MEDITERRANEAN SEA

F A C T · F I N D E R

When the volcano on the Greek island of Santorini erupted over 3,000 years ago, it caused the GREATEST EXPLOSION anyone has ever heard.

The enormous House of the Republic in Romania has over 1,000 ROOMS. It has never been lived in, because Ceaucescu, the man it was built for, fell from power in 1990.

The theatre at Epidaurus was built over 2,000 YEARS AGO and is still used today. Can you spot it on the map?

0   100   200   300   km

0   100   200 miles

SCANDINAVIA

Most of the countries of Northern Europe lie near to the Arctic Circle, so they have the same kind of weather - short summers and long, freezing winters. Very few people live up in the far north of Norway, Sweden and Finland, where snow covers the ground for much of the year. Most of the population live in the warmer south, where the land is green with forests and farmland.

Colourful In The Cold

Lapland lies in the far north of Norway, Sweden and Finland. The people who live there are called Lapps. They wear colourful woollen clothes and reindeer-skin boots to keep them warm in the icy winters.

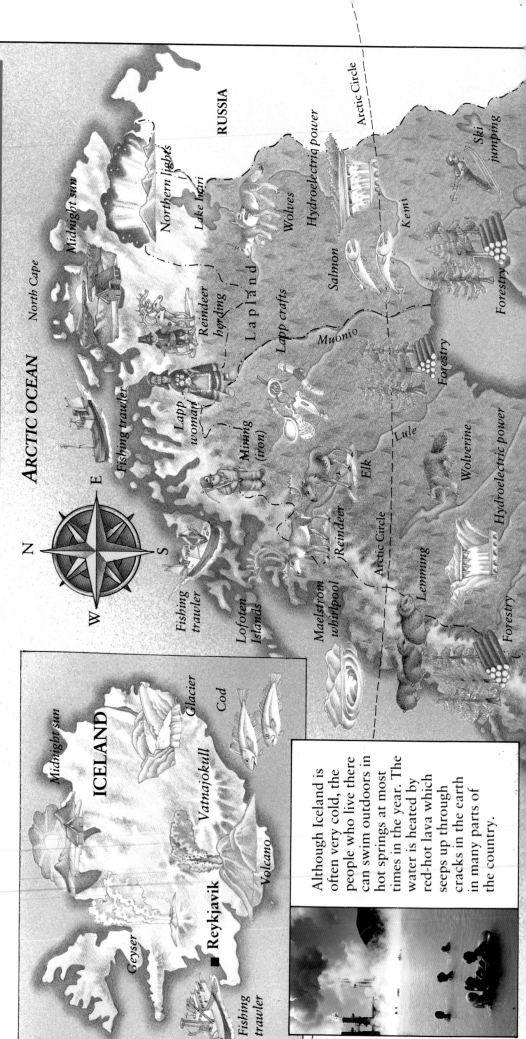

ARCTIC OCEAN

Midnight sun

North Cape

Northern lights

Lake Inari

RUSSIA

Arctic Circle

Hydroelectric power

Ski jumping

Wolves

Salmon

Kemi

Forestry

Reindeer herding

L a p l a n d

Lapp crafts

Muonio

Forestry

Fishing trawler

Lapp woman

Mining (iron)

Lule

Elk

Wolverine

Hydroelectric power

N
E
S
W

Fishing trawler

Reindeer

Arctic Circle

Lemming

Forestry

Lofoten Islands

Maelstrom whirlpool

Midnight sun

ICELAND

Glacier

Cod

Vatnajokull

Volcano

Reykjavik

Geyser

Fishing trawler

Although Iceland is often very cold, the people who live there can swim outdoors in hot springs at most times in the year. The water is heated by red-hot lava which seeps up through cracks in the earth in many parts of the country.

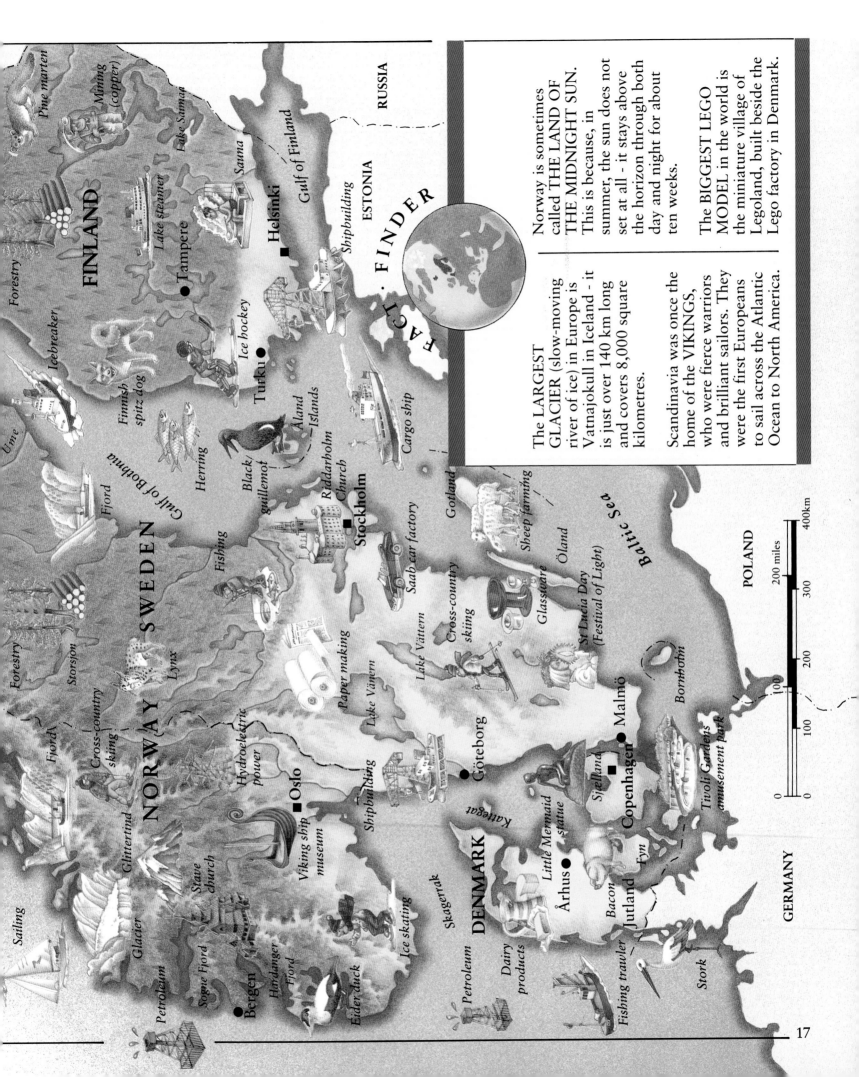

FINLAND

Pine marten

Mining (copper)

Lake Saimaa

Forestry

Lake steamer

Sauna

Tampere

Helsinki

Gulf of Finland

Shipbuilding

ESTONIA

RUSSIA

Icebreaker

Ice hockey

Turku

Finnish spitz dog

Åland Islands

Cargo ship

Ume

Herring

Black guillemot

Riddarholm Church

Fjord

Gulf of Bothnia

Stockholm

Gotland

Saab car factory

Sheep farming

Öland

Glassware

FINDER · FACT

Baltic Sea

Forestry

Storsjön

Lynx

SWEDEN

NORWAY

Paper making

Lake Vänern

Lake Vättern

Cross-country skiing

St Lucia Day (Festival of Light)

Glittertind

Cross-country skiing

Hydroelectric power

Oslo

Shipbuilding

Göteborg

Bornholm

Sailing

Fjord

Stave church

Viking ship museum

Kattegat

Copenhagen

Malmö

Tivoli Gardens amusement park

Glacier

Petroleum

Bergen

Sogne Fjord

Hardanger Fjord

Eider duck

Ice skating

Skagerrak

DENMARK

Little Mermaid statue

Århus

Sjælland

Fyn

Petroleum

Dairy products

Bacon

Jutland

Fishing trawler

Stork

GERMANY

POLAND

0   100   200   300   400km

0   100   200 miles

Norway is sometimes called THE LAND OF THE MIDNIGHT SUN. This is because, in summer, the sun does not set at all - it stays above the horizon through both day and night for about ten weeks.

The LARGEST GLACIER (slow-moving river of ice) in Europe is Vatnajokull in Iceland - it is just over 140 km long and covers 8,000 square kilometres.

Scandinavia was once the home of the VIKINGS, who were fierce warriors and brilliant sailors. They were the first Europeans to sail across the Atlantic Ocean to North America.

The BIGGEST LEGO MODEL in the world is the miniature village of Legoland, built beside the Lego factory in Denmark.

17

RUSSIA AND NEIGHBOURS

The Ural Mountains divide Russia into two. Most cities and farms are west and south of the Urals and most people live here. Siberia to the east is cold and bleak. A huge forest of fir and pine trees covers much of the north. South of it lies a vast, grassy plain called the steppes.

FACT · FINDER

Russia is the LARGEST COUNTRY in the world. It is nearly twice as big as Canada, the second largest.

Russia is so WIDE it takes 7 days to travel across it on the Trans-Siberian railway.

REINDEERS really do pull sledges in the snowy lands of the far north.

Lake Baikal is the world's DEEPEST lake. You could sink five Empire State buildings in it, one on top of the other.

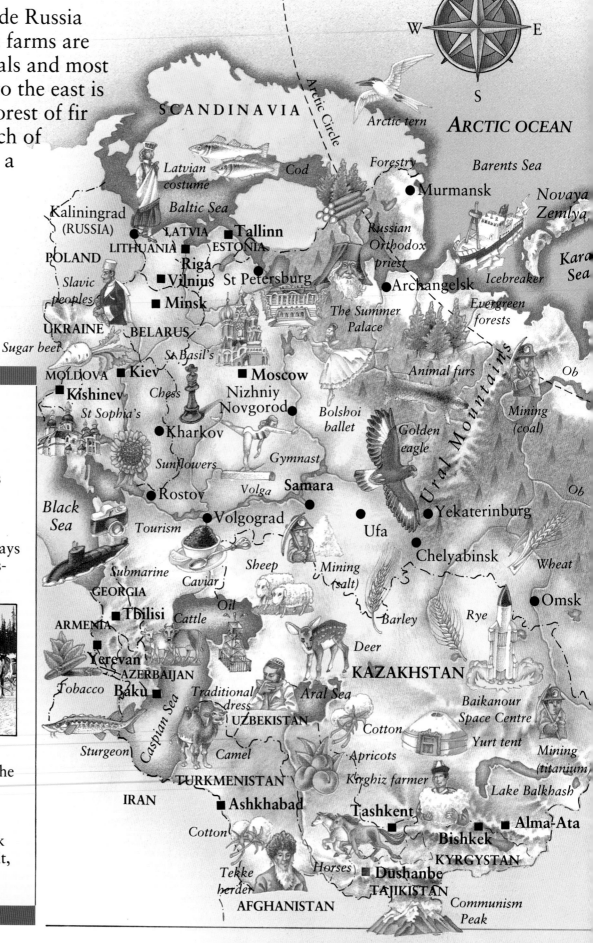

SCANDINAVIA

Arctic Circle

Arctic tern

ARCTIC OCEAN

Forestry

Barents Sea

Novaya Zemlya

Murmansk

Latvian costume

Cod

Baltic Sea

Russian Orthodox priest

Icebreaker

Kara Sea

Kaliningrad (RUSSIA)

POLAND

LATVIA

Tallinn

ESTONIA

LITHUANIA

Riga

St Petersburg

Archangelsk

Evergreen forests

Slavic peoples

Vilnius

Minsk

The Summer Palace

UKRAINE

BELARUS

St Basil's

Animal furs

Ural Mountains

Ob

Sugar beet

MOLDOVA

Kiev

Moscow

Mining (coal)

Kishinev

Chess

Nizhniy Novgorod

Bolshoi ballet

Golden eagle

St Sophia's

Kharkov

Gymnast

Sunflowers

Volga

Samara

Ob

Black Sea

Rostov

Yekaterinburg

Tourism

Volgograd

Ufa

Chelyabinsk

Wheat

Submarine

Caviar

Sheep

Mining (salt)

Barley

Rye

Omsk

GEORGIA

Tbilisi

Cattle

Oil

Deer

KAZAKHSTAN

ARMENIA

Yerevan

AZERBAIJAN

Baku

Caspian Sea

Traditional dress

Aral Sea

Baikanour Space Centre

Yurt tent

Mining (titanium)

Tobacco

UZBEKISTAN

Cotton

Lake Balkhash

Sturgeon

Camel

Apricots

Kirghiz farmer

TURKMENISTAN

IRAN

Ashkhabad

Cotton

Tashkent

Alma-Ata

Bishkek

KYRGYSTAN

Tekke herder

Horses

Dushanbe

TAJIKISTAN

Communism Peak

AFGHANISTAN

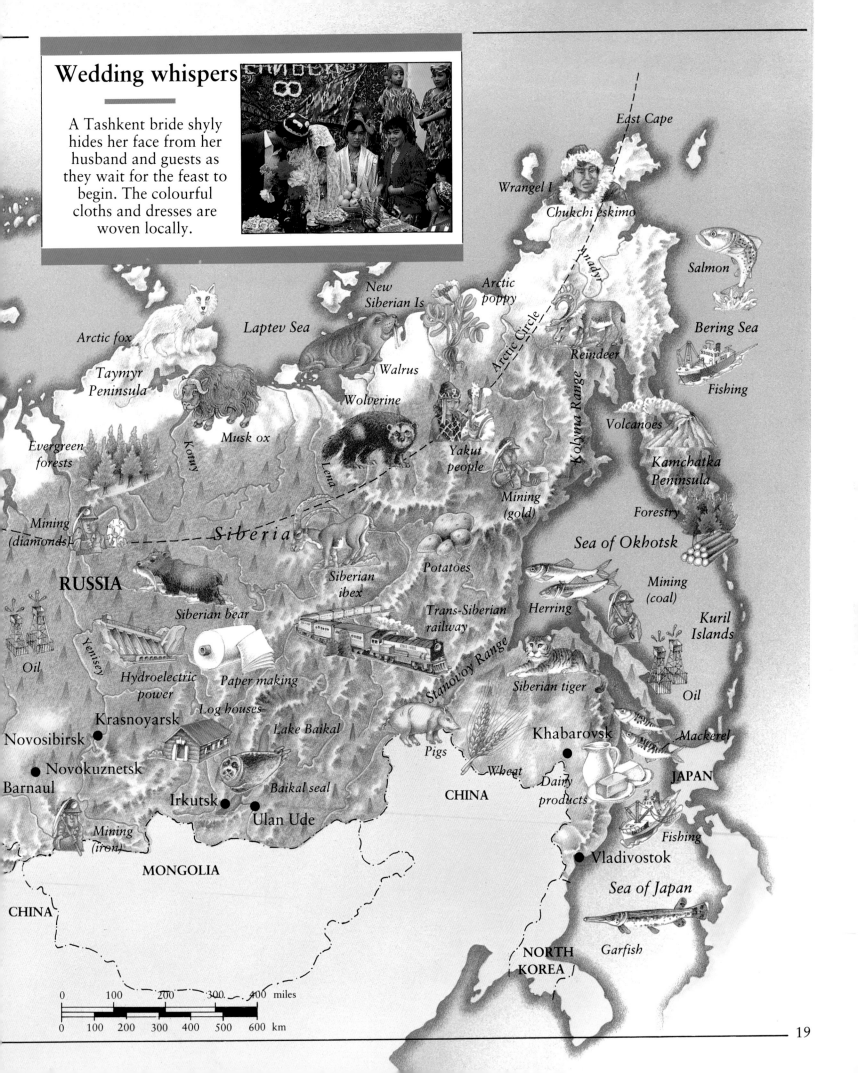

Wedding whispers

A Tashkent bride shyly hides her face from her husband and guests as they wait for the feast to begin. The colourful cloths and dresses are woven locally.

East Cape

Wrangel I

Chukchi eskimo

Arctic poppy

Arctic Circle

Anadyr

Salmon

New Siberian Is

Laptev Sea

Arctic fox

Taymyr Peninsula

Walrus

Wolverine

Reindeer

Bering Sea

Fishing

Kolyma Range

Musk ox

Evergreen forests

Kotuy

Lena

Yakut people

Volcanoes

Kamchatka Peninsula

Mining (diamonds)

Siberia

Mining (gold)

Forestry

Sea of Okhotsk

RUSSIA

Siberian ibex

Potatoes

Mining (coal)

Siberian bear

Trans-Siberian railway

Herring

Kuril Islands

Yenisey

Oil

Hydroelectric power

Paper making

Stanovoy Range

Siberian tiger

Oil

Krasnoyarsk

Log houses

Lake Baikal

Mackerel

Novosibirsk

Pigs

Wheat

Khabarovsk

Novokuznetsk

Baikal seal

Dairy products

JAPAN

Barnaul

Irkutsk

CHINA

Ulan Ude

Mining (iron)

Fishing

MONGOLIA

Vladivostok

CHINA

Sea of Japan

NORTH KOREA

Garfish

0   100   200   300   400 miles

0 100 200 300 400 500 600 km

THE MIDDLE EAST

Much of the Middle East has hot, dry weather for most of the year. There are hundreds of miles of sandy desert, where very little can survive in the blistering heat. Huge oilfields lie underneath some of these deserts, and under the waters of the Gulf. Countries like Saudi Arabia and Qatar have become very rich by pumping the oil from the ground and selling it to other countries all over the world.

BULGARIA
Ferry
Black Sea
Kebabs
Istanbul ●
Bosporus Monument
TURKEY
■ **Ankara**
GREECE
Ruins of Ephesus
Izmir ●
Whirling dervish
Taurus Mts
Adana ●
Cedar trees
Aleppo
SYRIA
Sponge diver
Cyprus
MEDITERRANEAN SEA
Grapefruit
LEBANON
Beirut ■
Damascus ■
Windsurfing
ISRAEL
wearing
Jerusalem ■ ■ Amman
JORDAN
EGYPT
Wailing Wall
Ruins of Petra
Irrigation
Cormorant
Oil
Tropic of Cancer
Royal Palace
Red Sea
SUDAN
Jidd
Golden Anthias fish
ERITREA
ETHIOPIA

A Syrian girl steals a kiss from her new sister.

Look, no hands - floating is easy on the salty Dead Sea.

FACT · FINDER

The LOWEST POINT on Earth is on the shore of the salty Dead Sea in Israel. It is 399 m below the water level of the world's oceans.

About a QUARTER of the world's entire oil reserves are found underneath Saudi Arabia.

Temperatures in the HOTTEST capital city in the world can reach 40°C in the summer. It is in the largest country on this map. Can you see which one? (Answer: page 48)

One of the OLDEST capital cities in the world is Damascus in Syria. It was founded about 5,000 years ago.

The city of Jerusalem is regarded as a HOLY PLACE for members of three of the world's major religions - Christians, Muslims and Jews.

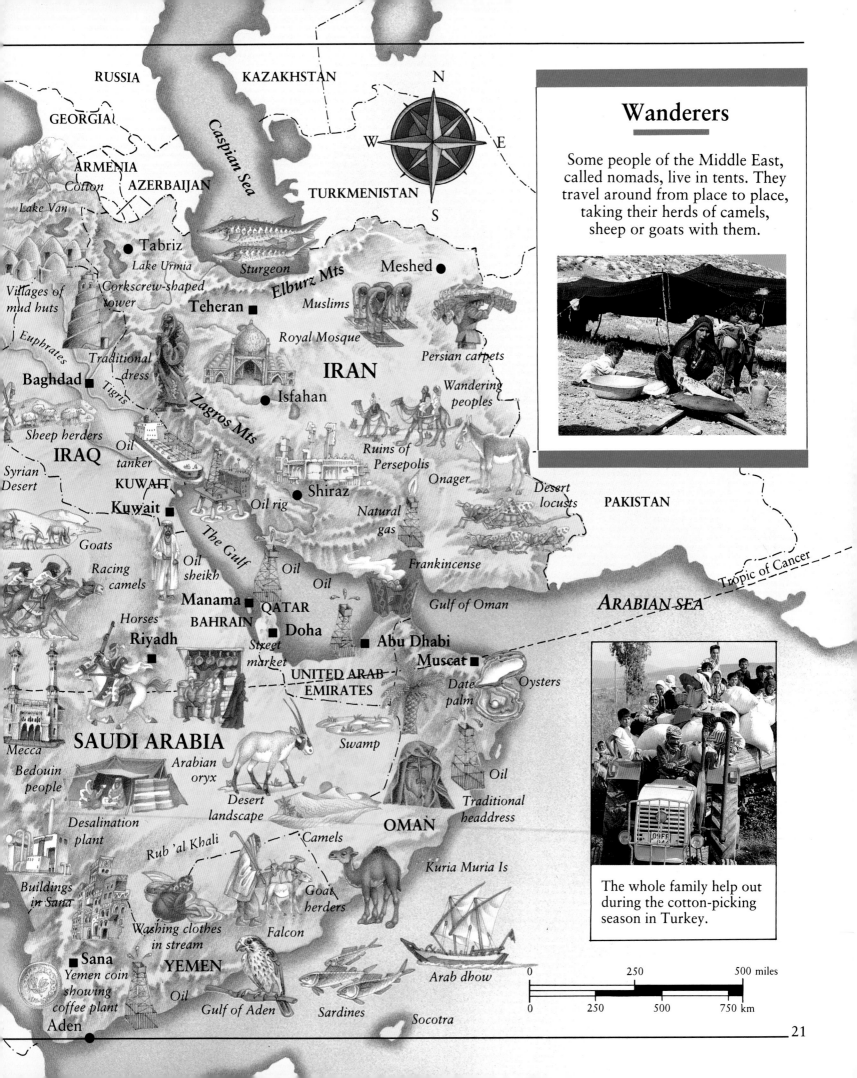

RUSSIA

KAZAKHSTAN

GEORGIA

ARMENIA

AZERBAIJAN

TURKMENISTAN

Cotton

Lake Van

Caspian Sea

N
W · E
S

Tabriz

Lake Urmia

Sturgeon

Elburz Mts

Meshed

Villages of mud huts

Corkscrew-shaped tower

Teheran

Muslims

Royal Mosque

Euphrates

Traditional dress

IRAN

Persian carpets

Baghdad

Tigris

Zagros Mts

Isfahan

Wandering peoples

Sheep herders

Oil tanker

IRAQ

Ruins of Persepolis

Onager

Syrian Desert

KUWAIT

Shiraz

Desert locusts

PAKISTAN

Kuwait

Oil rig

Natural gas

Goats

The Gulf

Racing camels

Oil sheikh

Oil

Frankincense

Gulf of Oman

Tropic of Cancer

ARABIAN SEA

Oil

Manama

QATAR

Horses

BAHRAIN

Doha

Abu Dhabi

Riyadh

Street market

Muscat

UNITED ARAB EMIRATES

Date palm

Oysters

SAUDI ARABIA

Arabian oryx

Swamp

Oil

Mecca

Bedouin people

Traditional headdress

Desert landscape

OMAN

Desalination plant

Rub 'al Khali

Camels

Buildings in Sana

Kuria Muria Is

Washing clothes in stream

Goat herders

Falcon

Sana

Yemen coin showing coffee plant

Arab dhow

Oil

YEMEN

Gulf of Aden

Sardines

Socotra

Aden

Wanderers

Some people of the Middle East, called nomads, live in tents. They travel around from place to place, taking their herds of camels, sheep or goats with them.

The whole family help out during the cotton-picking season in Turkey.

0   250   500 miles

0   250   500   750 km

21

SOUTH ASIA

South Asia is one of the world's most crowded places. It is usually hot and humid, but has a very rainy season called the monsoon. It is home to many wild creatures, such as tigers and elephants, and has the world's highest mountain, Mount Everest, in the Himalayas.

The HIGHEST MOUNTAIN in the world is Mount Everest on the Nepal-Tibet border in the Himalayas. It is 8,848 metres high. The Himalaya-Karakoram range has 96 peaks that are over 7,300 metres.

One of the most BEAUTIFUL BUILDINGS in the world is the tomb known as the Taj Mahal. It was built by a ruler of India in memory of his favourite wife. It took 20,000 workers 20 years to build it.

The Ganges is one of the LONGEST RIVERS in the world. It starts in an ice cave, over 3,000 m up in the Himalaya mountains. Can you see where it ends? (Answer: page 48)

DANGEROUS ANIMALS! People who live outside the towns sometimes have to worry about such creatures as crocodiles, leopards, rhinoceroses, scorpions, tigers, and poisonous snakes.

Fathers in Bhutan often carry their children around on their backs like this.

A snake has no ears, so it cannot hear. It is the rhythmic, swaying movements of the charmer, not the music of his flute, that makes the snake raise its head and neck from the basket to watch.

N
E
W
S

CHINA

Himalaya Mountains

Street market

Mount Godwin-Austen (K2)

Woman wearing sari

Kashmir

Irrigation

Lahore

Islamabad

Khyber Pass

Hindu Kush

Muslim at prayer

TAJIKISTAN

UZBEKISTAN

TURKMENISTAN

Blue mosque

Kabul

Mining (Lapis lazuli)

AFGHANISTAN

Goat

IRAN

Wheat

Camel transport

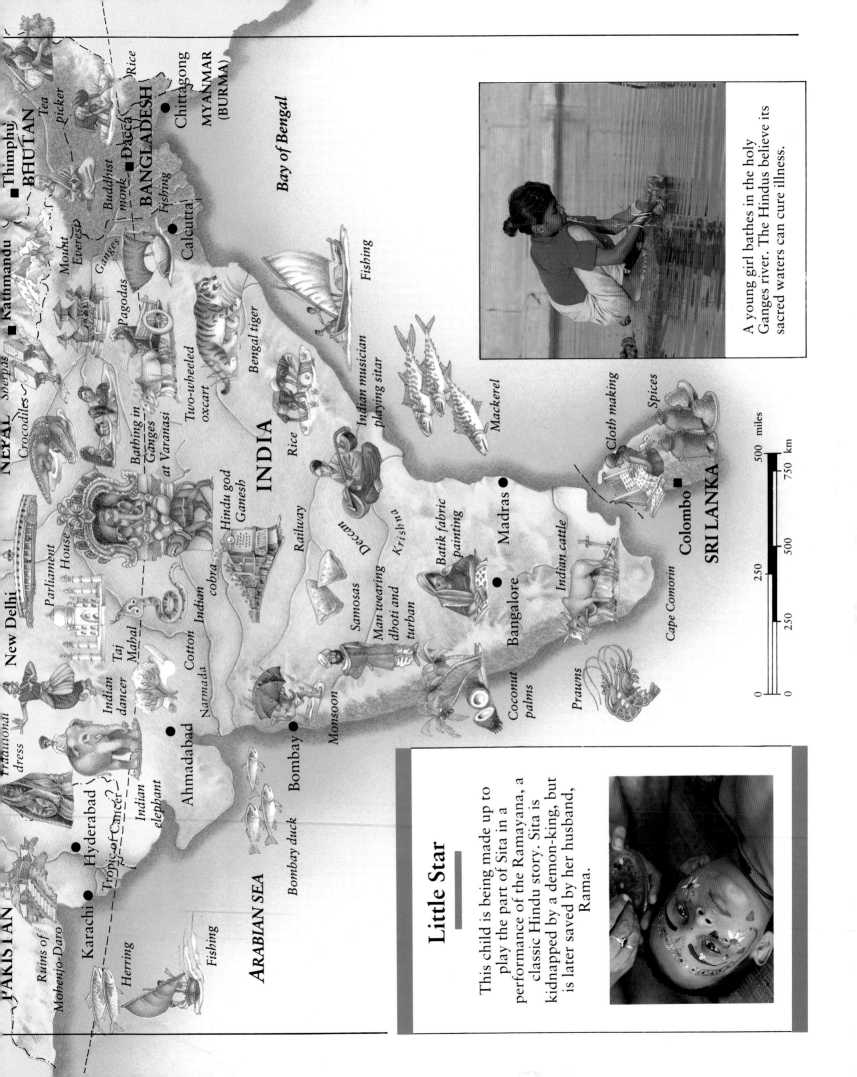

A young girl bathes in the holy Ganges river. The Hindus believe its sacred waters can cure illness.

Little Star

This child is being made up to play the part of Sita in a performance of the Ramayana, a classic Hindu story. Sita is kidnapped by a demon-king, but is later saved by her husband, Rama.

EASTERN ASIA

Eastern Asia has many different kinds of landscape. It includes high mountains, like those in Tibet, and hot deserts, such as the Gobi, as well as huge plains where farmers grow rice, tea and other crops. China is by far the largest country in this area. Japan is made up of a group of islands - 4 main ones and about 3,000 much smaller ones.

KAZAKHSTAN

Altai Mountains

Selenge

Nomadic herders

Sheep

Dzungarian Desert

Mining (coal)

Goats

MONGOLIA

Tian Shan

Turpan Depression

CHINA

Tea-picking

TAJIKISTAN

Musk deer

Taklimakan Desert

Yak

Monsoon

Giant panda

Przewalski's horse

Kunlun Mountains

Red panda

N
W — E
S

Yak

Oil

Mining (salt)

Musk perfume

Pagoda

Buddhist monk

Plateau of Tibet

Bicycles

INDIA

Carpet making

Tibetan terrier

Chengdu

Keep out!

A school trip visits the Great Wall of China. The wall, which is over 6,000 km long, was built more than 2,000 years ago to protect China from enemies.

Himalaya

NEPAL

Potala Palace

Mountains

Barley

Yalong

BHUTAN

Bamboo

Lychees

Tropic of Cancer

Mekong

MYANMAR (BURMA)

LAOS

Mount Fuji, the highest peak in Japan, was once an active volcano.

RUSSIA

Rice farming

Horses

Manchurian pine

Kerulen

● **Ulan Bator**

Camels

Gobi Desert

Sweet potatoes

Manchuria ● Harbin

RUSSIA

Kimonos

Hokkaido
● Sapporo

Softball

Changchun
●

Porcelain

Rice farming

Sea of Japan

Fishing

JAPAN

Sumo wrestling

Honshu

● Shenyang

NORTH KOREA

Oysters

Great Wall of China

Soybeans

Golden pheasant

■ **Beijing**
● Tianjin

Mining (silver)

■ **Pyongyang**

■ **Seoul**

Car factories

■ **Tokyo**
Yokohama

Mulberries

Kyoto
Kobe
● Nagoya
Osaka

Tai Chi exercise

● Taiyuan

● Zibo

Loquat tree

Yellow Sea

SOUTH KOREA

Korea Strait

Shikoku

Kyushu

Electronics

Fishing

● Xi'an

Rice farming

● Zhengzhou

Grand Canal

Pollack

PACIFIC OCEAN

Terracotta Army

Yangtze

Silk painting

● Nanjing

● Shanghai

East China Sea

FACT · FINDER

● Chongqing

● Wuhan

Chinese musical instruments

Dongting Lake

Poyang Lake

Fishing

Shrimp

Rice farming

Noodles

Formosa Strait

■ **Taipei**

Tropic of Cancer

China is the country with the LARGEST POPULATION in the world - just over 1.1 billion. This is about one-fifth of all the people alive today.

Opium poppy

● Guangzhou

TAIWAN

The BIGGEST CITY in this area is Tokyo, with nearly 12 million people.

Xi Jiang

Spices

◉ Hong Kong

● Macao

Tuna

VIETNAM

Hainan Island

Fishing

South China Sea

0   100   200   300   400 miles

0   200   400   600 km

Japan has the LONGEST RAILWAY TUNNEL in the world. It is over 50 km long, and almost half of it runs deep under the sea.

SOUTHEAST ASIA

Southeast Asia is very hot and often very wet. The tropical rainforests are being cleared for farmland and fast-growing towns. But there are some National Parks where trees and wildlife are protected. Some mountains are volcanoes: there are 77 active ones in Indonesia! In the Philippines, 250,000 people had to flee from Mount Pinatubo in 1991-92.

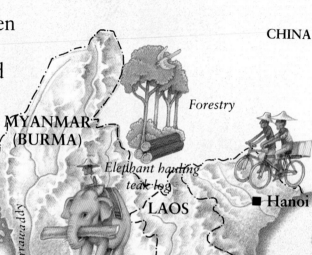

CHINA

Forestry

MYANMAR (BURMA)

Elephant hauling teak log

Cyclists

LAOS

■ **Hanoi**

Irrawaddy

■ **Vientiane**

Rangoon ■

Rice farming

Chinese junk

Tourism

THAILAND

Bangkok ■

CAMBODIA (KAMPUCHEA)

Angkor Wat

Andaman Islands

VIETNAM

Spanish mackerel

Floating market

Phnom Penh ■

Tourism

● **Ho Chi Minh City**

Drying fish

Container ship

Rubber trees

Rubber trees

MALAYSIA

Bandar Seri Begawan ■
BRUNEI

Rubber trees
Medan ●

Kuala Lumpur ■

Skyscrapers

Orang-uta...

Oil

■ **SINGAPORE**

Rubber trees

Giant flowers

Sumatra

INDONESIA

INDIAN OCEAN

Bangka

Borneo

Coffee

Tiger

Borobudur Temple

■ **Jakarta**

Semarang ●

Surabaya

● **Bandung**

Java *Tourism*

Bali

Fishing

Batik cloth

Shadow Puppets

Puppet shows are popular in Indonesia. Amazing puppets are held up on sticks behind a white screen. The audience sees their shadows in front of a bright light. Perhaps you can make your own shadow-puppet show.

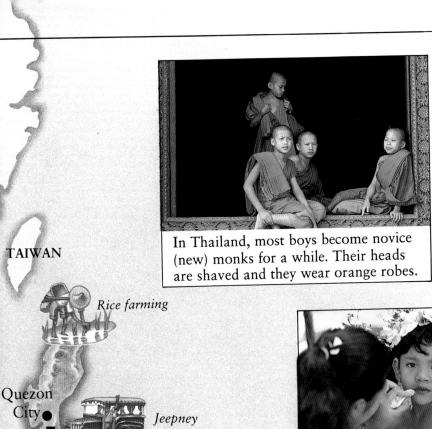

In Thailand, most boys become novice (new) monks for a while. Their heads are shaved and they wear orange robes.

TAIWAN

Rice farming

Quezon City

Manila

Jeepney

THE PHILIPPINES

Stilt houses

Tasaday tribe

A special day in Myanmar (Burma): this girl is getting ready for a village procession.

The HIGHEST MOUNTAIN in this area is Hkakabo Razi in Burma (Myanmar) - it is 5,881 metres high.

The LONGEST RIVER is the Mekong - 4,180 kilometres long, the 12th longest river in the world.

Of all the countries on this map, INDONESIA has by far the most people; it has the 4th biggest population in the world.

The BIGGEST CITY is Jakarta, capital of Indonesia - over 7 million people live there.

MONEY TO SPEND ... in Vietnam, the money you spend is called a DONG. In Laos it is called a KIP.

MAKING SENSE OF BORNEO: The island of Borneo has PARTS of TWO countries and the WHOLE of ONE country. Can you see which they are? (Answer: page 48)

PACIFIC OCEAN

Coral reefs

Oil

Tuna

Equator

Toraja house

Halmahera

Sulawesi (Celebes)

Moluccas

Coffee

Irian Jaya

Volcanoes

PAPUA NEW GUINEA

Banda Sea

Komodo dragon

Sharks

Bird of paradise

| 0 | 100 | 200 | 300 | 400 | 500 miles |

| 0 | 250 | 500 | 750 km |

Timor

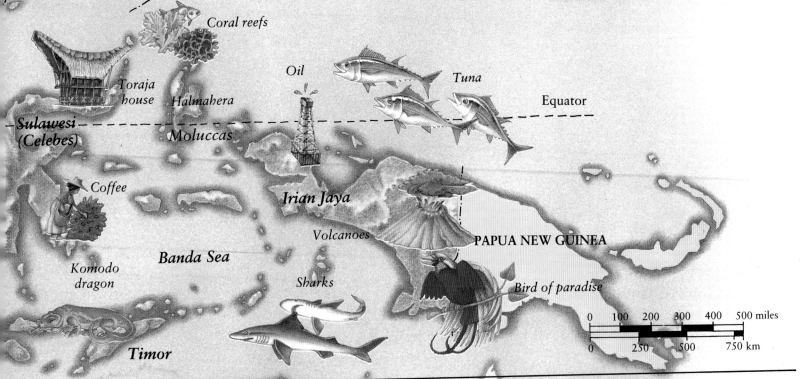

AUSTRALIA

27

NORTHERN AFRICA

The Sahara Desert covers most of North Africa. It is scorching hot in daytime but cold at night. Plants and crops grow around the coast and along the banks of the River Nile. Steamy rainforest once stretched from Sierra Leone to Cameroon, but most of the trees have been cut down to make room for cocoa, coffee and other crops.

FACT · FINDER

The Sahara Desert is the LARGEST DESERT and it is getting bigger. It spreads at the rate of a football pitch every 15 seconds.

Massive stone statues guard the ancient temple of Abu Simbel. During the mid-1960s, in an amazing FEAT OF ENGINEERING, the whole structure was moved, piece by piece, up onto higher ground. This was to make way for the huge reservoir now known as Lake Nasser.

FRANCE

SPAIN

PORTUGAL

Shrimp

Algiers

Couscous

Rabat ● Fez
Casablanca
MOROCCO *Atlas Mountains*

Oil

Marrakesh

ATLANTIC OCEAN

Berber women

Scorpion

S a h a r a

ALGERIA

Camel caravan

Canary Islands (Spain) *Tourism*
Sardines
Las Palmas

Addax antelope

El Aaiún

WESTERN SAHARA

Tropic of Cancer

Mining (iron)

Jackal

Nomadic herders

Mining (uranium)

MALI

Sankore mosque, Timbuktu

Nomad camp

MAURITANIA

Fishing from beach

Nouakchott

SENEGAL

Peanuts

Slender-snouted crocodile

Ancient Nok civilisation

Dakar

GAMBIA

Banjul

Hyena

Giraffe

Dogon dancer

Niamey

Bissau

GUINEA-BISSAU

Bamako

Ouagadougou

BURKINA FASO

Conakry

Mud hut village

GHANA

BENIN

Yams

GUINEA

SIERRA LEONE

Freetown

Lake Volta

Abu

Dian monk

Porto-Novo

Pygmy hippopotamus

IVORY COAST

TOGO

Monrovia

Accra **Lomé** **Lagos**

LIBERIA **Abidjan**

Tuna

Shrimp

ATLANTIC OCEAN

Equator

Lomé cathedral

Oil

0	200	400	600	800	1000 miles

0	400	800	1200	1600 km

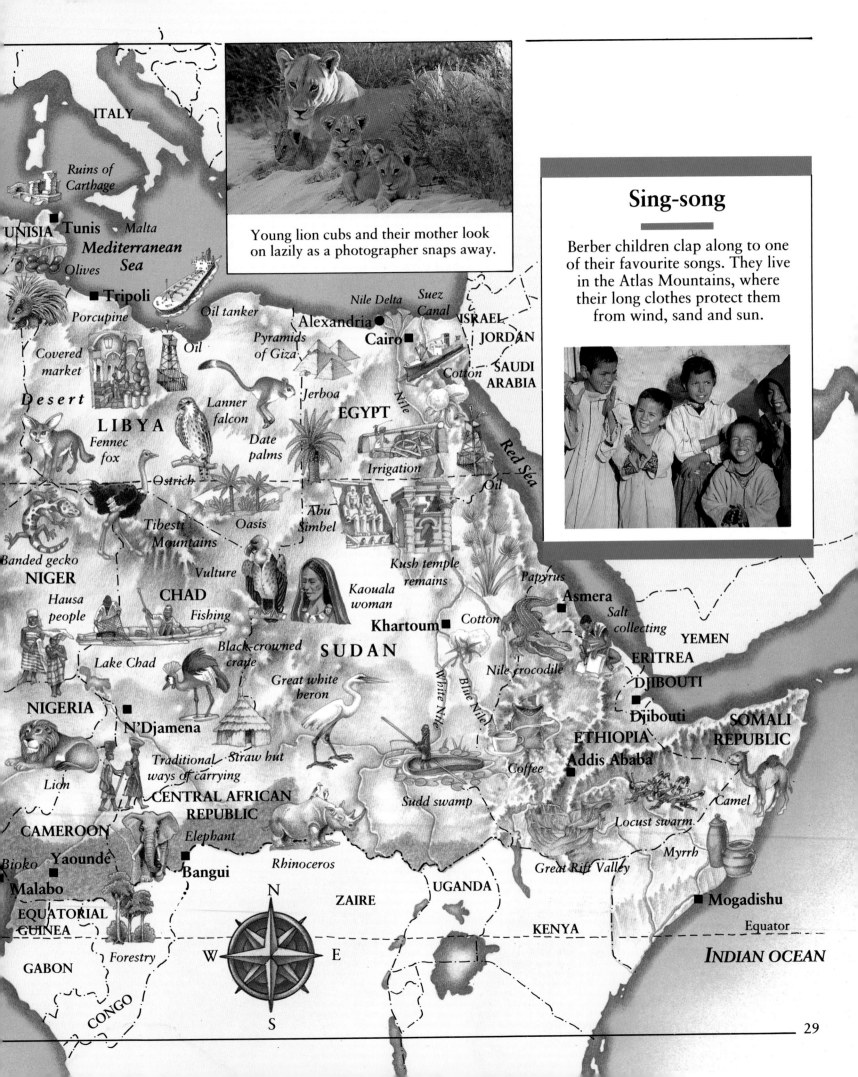

ITALY

Ruins of Carthage

TUNISIA **Tunis** *Malta*

Mediterranean Sea

Olives

Tripoli *Oil tanker* *Nile Delta* *Suez Canal* ISRAEL

Porcupine *Oil* **Alexandria** JORDAN

Covered market *Pyramids of Giza* **Cairo** SAUDI ARABIA

Desert *Oil* *Cotton*

Fennec fox **LIBYA** *Lanner falcon* *Jerboa* **EGYPT**

Date palms

Ostrich *Irrigation* *Nile*

Banded gecko *Tibesti Mountains* *Oasis* *Abu Simbel* *Red Sea*

NIGER *Vulture* *Kush temple remains* *Papyrus*

Hausa people **CHAD** *Kaouala woman* **Asmera** *Salt collecting*

Fishing *Cotton* YEMEN

Lake Chad **Khartoum** *Nile crocodile* **ERITREA**

NIGERIA *Black-crowned crane* **SUDAN** **DJIBOUTI**

N'Djamena *Great white heron* **Djibouti** **SOMALI REPUBLIC**

Straw hut *White Nile* *Blue Nile* **ETHIOPIA**

Lion *Traditional ways of carrying* *Coffee* **Addis Ababa**

CENTRAL AFRICAN REPUBLIC *Sudd swamp* *Camel*

CAMEROON *Elephant* *Locust swarm*

Bioko **Yaoundé** *Rhinoceros* *Myrrh*

Malabo **Bangui** UGANDA *Great Rift Valley*

EQUATORIAL GUINEA **ZAIRE** N **Mogadishu**

GABON *Forestry* KENYA *Equator*

W E

CONGO S ***INDIAN OCEAN***

Young lion cubs and their mother look on lazily as a photographer snaps away.

Sing-song

Berber children clap along to one of their favourite songs. They live in the Atlas Mountains, where their long clothes protect them from wind, sand and sun.

29

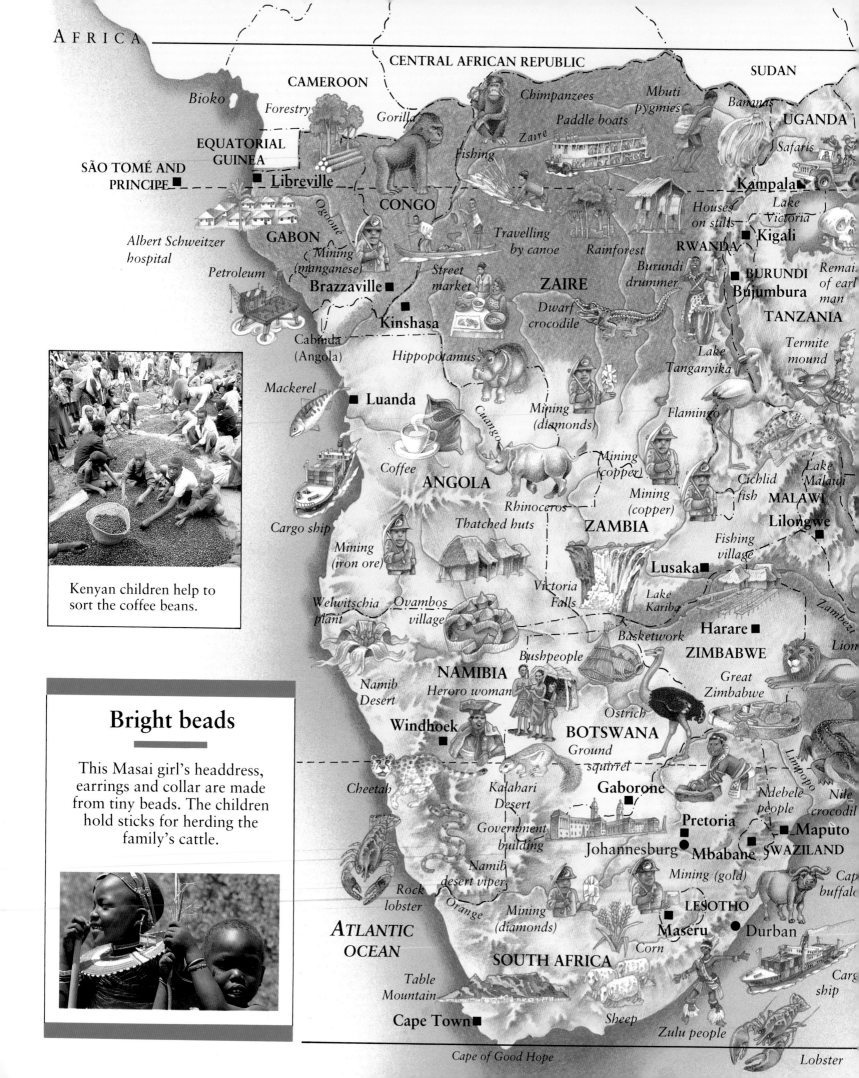

CENTRAL AFRICAN REPUBLIC

SUDAN

CAMEROON

Bioko

Forestry

Gorilla

Chimpanzees

Mbuti pygmies

Bananas

Paddle boats

UGANDA

Zaïre

Fishing

Safaris

EQUATORIAL GUINEA

SÃO TOMÉ AND PRINCIPE ■

Libreville ■

Kampala ■

CONGO

Street market

Houses on stills

Kigali ■

Lake Victoria

Ogooué

GABON

RWANDA

Mining (manganese)

Travelling by canoe

Rainforest

Burundi drummer

■ BURUNDI

Remains of early man

Albert Schweitzer hospital

Petroleum

Bujumbura

Brazzaville ■

ZAÏRE

TANZANIA

■ Kinshasa

Dwarf crocodile

Lake Tanganyika

Termite mound

Cabinda (Angola)

Hippopotamus

Kenyan children help to sort the coffee beans.

Mackerel

Luanda ■

Mining (diamonds)

Flamingo

Coffee

Mining (copper)

Cichlid fish

Lake Malawi

ANGOLA

Rhinoceros

Mining (copper)

MALAWI

Cargo ship

Thatched huts

ZAMBIA

Lilongwe ■

Mining (iron ore)

Fishing village

Lusaka ■

Bright beads

This Masai girl's headdress, earrings and collar are made from tiny beads. The children hold sticks for herding the family's cattle.

Welwitschia plant

Ovambos village

Victoria Falls

Lake Kariba

Zambezi

Basketwork

Harare ■

Bushpeople

ZIMBABWE

Lion

Namib Desert

NAMIBIA

Heroro woman

Great Zimbabwe

Ostrich

Windhoek ■

BOTSWANA

Ground squirrel

Ndebele people

Nile crocodile

Cheetah

Kalahari Desert

Gaborone ■

Pretoria ■

■ Maputo

Government building

Johannesburg ●

Mbabane ●

SWAZILAND

Namib desert viper

Mining (gold)

Cape buffalo

Rock lobster

Orange

Mining (diamonds)

LESOTHO

ATLANTIC OCEAN

Corn

Maseru ■

● Durban

SOUTH AFRICA

Table Mountain

Sheep

Cape Town ■

Zulu people

Cargo ship

Cape of Good Hope

Lobster

SOUTHERN AFRICA

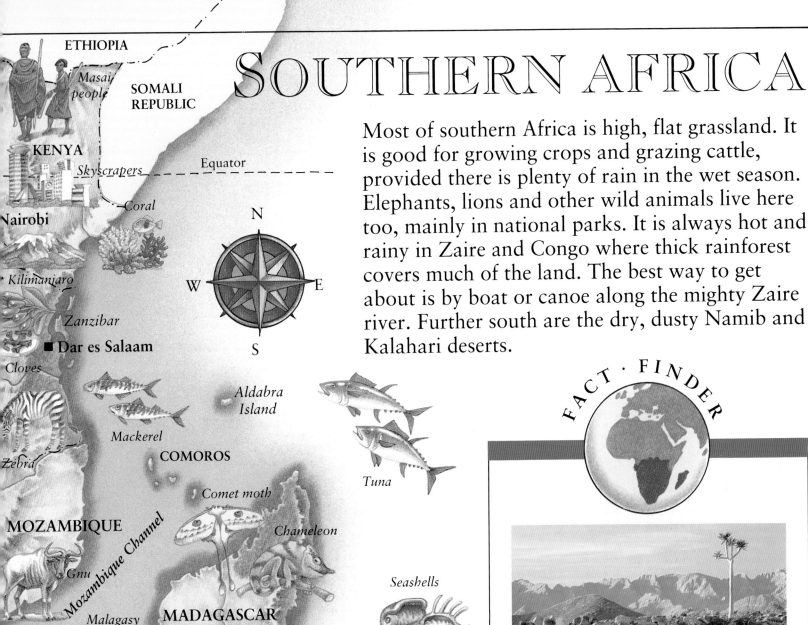

ETHIOPIA

Masai people

SOMALI REPUBLIC

KENYA

Skyscrapers

Equator

Coral

Nairobi

Kilimanjaro

Zanzibar

■ **Dar es Salaam**

Cloves

N

W   E

S

Mackerel

Aldabra Island

Zebra

COMOROS

Comet moth

MOZAMBIQUE

Mozambique Channel

Chameleon

Gnu

Malagasy people

MADAGASCAR

■

Antananarivo

Vanilla

Shrimp

Zebu cattle and cart

Tropic of Capricorn

Lemur

Tuna

Seashells

MAURITIUS

Reunion

Sardines

INDIAN OCEAN

0	200	400 miles
0	400	800 km

Most of southern Africa is high, flat grassland. It is good for growing crops and grazing cattle, provided there is plenty of rain in the wet season. Elephants, lions and other wild animals live here too, mainly in national parks. It is always hot and rainy in Zaire and Congo where thick rainforest covers much of the land. The best way to get about is by boat or canoe along the mighty Zaire river. Further south are the dry, dusty Namib and Kalahari deserts.

FACT · FINDER

FEW TREES grow in the dry, stony land of the Karroo in South Africa.

The top of Mount Kilimanjaro is the COLDEST PLACE in Africa. It is so high, it is always covered with snow.

The LARGEST UNCUT DIAMOND was found in South Africa. It was as large as a grapefruit.

Great Zimbabwe was once the capital of powerful AFRICAN CHIEFS. Can you see it on the map?

A chimp takes time out from his busy day to sit and think.

CANADA

Most of Canada is a vast wilderness of ice and snow, forests and lakes. Many wild animals live here and in the Rocky Mountains, but few people can survive. Farmers herd cattle and grow huge fields of wheat on the grassy prairies east of the Rockies, but most people live in the big cities near the United States border.

A brown bear snatches a fish with its huge front paw.

Night sky spectacle

If you are quite far north or south on the Earth, you can sometimes see strange, coloured lights in the night sky. These are known as the *Aurora borealis* in the north and *Aurora australis* in the south.

ARCTIC OCEAN

Migrating King eider ducks

Beaufort Sea

Queen Elizabeth Islands

Alaska (US)

Banks Island

Snowy owl

Icebreaker

Arctic Circle

Mount Logan

Pink lousewort

Victoria Island

Mackenzie

Great Bear Lake

Arctic hare

Mining (zinc)

Motor tricycles

YUKON TERRITORY

NORTHWEST

Glaciers

Eskimo people

Ice safari

Great Slave Lake

Forestry

Polar bear

Indian ceremonial mask

Cargo barges

BRITISH COLUMBIA

Peace

Herring

Oil

Moose

Fraser

ALBERTA

Reindeer Lake

Nelson

Grizzly bear

Wheat

MANITOBA

Edmonton

Salmon

Cattle

The Royal Canadian Mounted Police

Lake Winnipeg

Vancouver

Calgary

SASKATCHEWAN

Perch

Vancouver harbour

Calgary Stampede

Winnipeg

THE UNITED STATES

Ice hockey

0	100	200	300	400	500 miles

0	200	400	600	800	1000 km

Ellesmere
Island

Devon
Island

Greenland

ICELAND

Baffin Bay

Caribou

Baffin
Island

Icebergs

Davis Strait

Arctic Circle

TERRITORIES

Arctic
buttercup

Bowhead whale

ATLANTIC OCEAN

Hudson Strait

Kittiwake

Bearded
seal

Cod

Hudson Bay

Mining
(iron ore)

Caribou

NEWFOUND-
LAND

Spruce
grouse

Hydroelectric
power

QUEBEC

Cargo ship

Cabot
tower

Fishing

ONTARIO

Forestry

Forestry

Château
Frontenac

Beaver

St Lawrence

Ringed seal

Newfoundland

PRINCE EDWARD
ISLAND

NEW
BRUNSWICK

Lake
Superior

Cargo ship

Bald
eagle

Quebec

Skiing

NOVA
SCOTIA

Lake
Huron

Montreal

CN Tower

Ottawa

THE UNITED
STATES

Scallops

ATLANTIC
OCEAN

Beluga

Maple
trees

Toronto

Lake
Ontario

Lake Erie

Lake Superior is the LARGEST
FRESHWATER LAKE in the world.
Ships sail up the St Lawrence river to the
Great Lakes. How many lakes would
you cross to reach Lake Superior?

The Inuits (Eskimos) have TWENTY
different words for snow.

The CN Tower in Toronto is the
TALLEST FREE-STANDING
BUILDING in the world. From the top,
you can see far beyond the city.

There are almost NO ROADS in
northern Canada, so people use AIR
TAXIS instead - small planes which can
take off and land on the lakes.

Playing ice hockey is a good way
to keep out the cold.

THE UNITED STATES

The United States of America is the fourth largest country in the world. It has thousands of miles of farmland, baking hot deserts, and huge, snow-topped mountains. It also has some enormous cities. The giant of them all is New York City, home to over 18 million people.

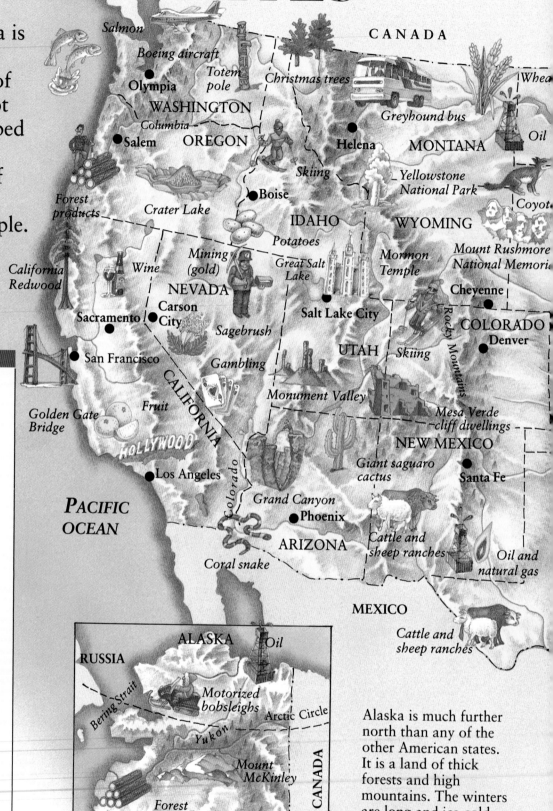

FACT · FINDER

The United States has more kilometres of roads and railways that any other country. The world's BUSIEST AIRPORT is in a city in the state of Illinois. Can you see it? (Answer: p48)

About 250 MILLION PEOPLE live in the United States.

There are 50 STATES altogether. There is also a special piece of land, the District of Columbia. This is where the capital city, Washington, D.C., is found.

Salmon
Boeing aircraft
Olympia
Totem pole
WASHINGTON
Columbia
Salem   OREGON
Forest products
Crater Lake
California Redwood
Wine
Sacramento   Carson City
NEVADA
San Francisco
Golden Gate Bridge
Fruit
HOLLYWOOD
Los Angeles
PACIFIC OCEAN
CALIFORNIA
Colorado
Coral snake

CANADA
Christmas trees
Helena
Skiing
Boise
IDAHO
Potatoes
Mining (gold)
Great Salt Lake
NEVADA
Sagebrush
Gambling
Monument Valley
UTAH
Grand Canyon
Phoenix
ARIZONA

Greyhound bus
MONTANA
Wheat
Oil
Yellowstone National Park
Coyote
WYOMING
Mormon Temple
Mount Rushmore National Memorial
Cheyenne
Salt Lake City
Skiing
Rocky Mountains
COLORADO
Denver
Mesa Verde cliff dwellings
NEW MEXICO
Giant saguaro cactus
Santa Fe
Cattle and sheep ranches
Oil and natural gas

MEXICO
Cattle and sheep ranches

Alaska inset map

ALASKA   Oil
RUSSIA
Bering Strait
Motorized bobsleighs
Arctic Circle
Yukon
Mount McKinley
CANADA
Forest products
Anchorage
Kodiak bear

0 100 200 300 miles
0   250   500 km

Alaska is much further north than any of the other American states. It is a land of thick forests and high mountains. The winters are long and ice-cold, with snow covering much of the ground. The people often travel around in sledges.

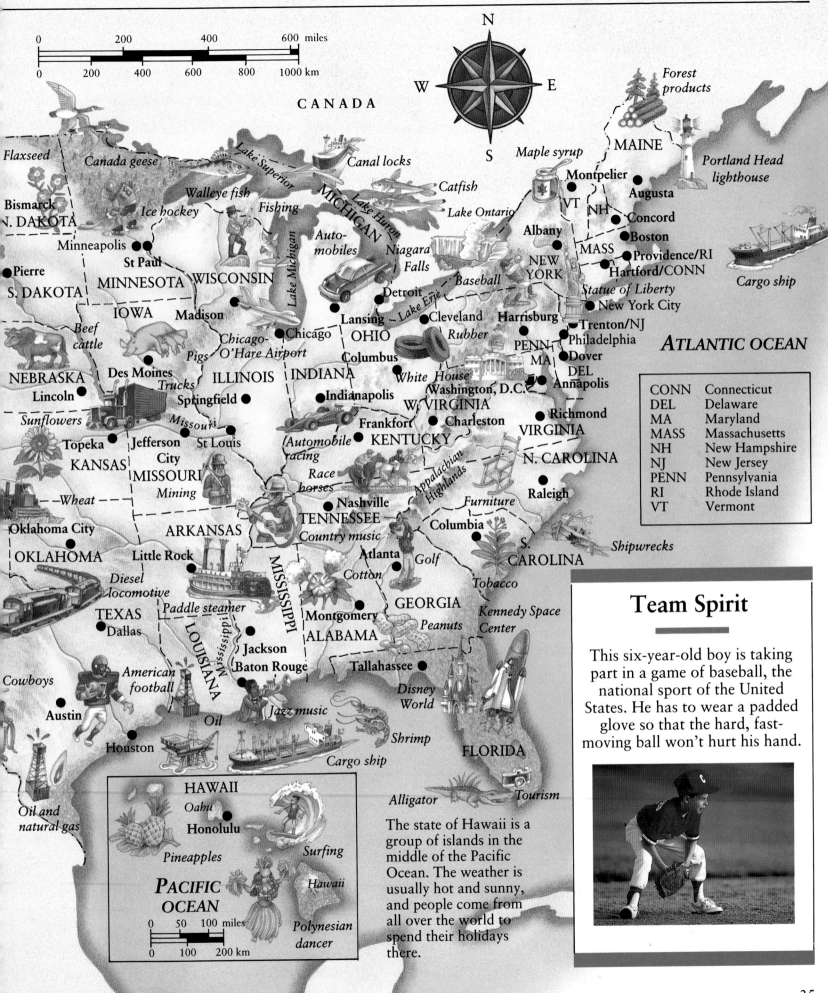

0   200   400   600 miles
0   200   400   600   800   1000 km

N
W   E
S

CANADA

Forest products

Flaxseed

Canada geese

Lake Superior   *Canal locks*

Maple syrup   MAINE

Walleye fish   MICHIGAN   Lake Huron   *Catfish*   **Montpelier**   *Portland Head lighthouse*

Bismarck   *Ice hockey*   *Fishing*   Lake Ontario   VT   NH   **Augusta**

N. DAKOTA   **Albany**   **Concord**

Auto-mobiles   *Niagara Falls*   NEW   **Boston**

Minneapolis   YORK   MASS   **Providence/RI**

St Paul   WISCONSIN   Lake Michigan   *Baseball*   **Hartford/CONN**

Pierre   MINNESOTA   *Statue of Liberty*   *Cargo ship*

S. DAKOTA   Lake Erie   **New York City**

IOWA   **Madison**   **Lansing**   **Cleveland**   **Harrisburg**   **Trenton/NJ**   **ATLANTIC OCEAN**

Beef cattle   Chicago-   **Chicago**   OHIO   *Rubber*   PENN   **Philadelphia**

Pigs   O'Hare Airport   **Columbus**   **Dover**   MA   DEL

NEBRASKA   **Des Moines**   *Trucks*   ILLINOIS   INDIANA   *White House*   **Annapolis**

Lincoln   **Springfield**   **Indianapolis**   **Washington, D.C.**

Sunflowers   *Missouri*   **Frankfort**   W. VIRGINIA   **Richmond**

Topeka   **Jefferson**   **St Louis**   *Automobile racing*   **Charleston**   VIRGINIA

KANSAS   **City**   KENTUCKY   **N. CAROLINA**

MISSOURI   *Race horses*   Appalachian   **Raleigh**

Wheat   *Mining*   Highlands   *Furniture*

Oklahoma City   **Nashville**   **Columbia**   S.

Little Rock   TENNESSEE   **CAROLINA**   *Shipwrecks*

OKLAHOMA   ARKANSAS   *Country music*   *Golf*

Diesel locomotive   *Atlanta*   *Tobacco*

Paddle steamer   MISSISSIPPI   *Cotton*   GEORGIA

TEXAS   **Montgomery**   *Peanuts*   *Kennedy Space Center*

Dallas   LOUISIANA   ALABAMA

Cowboys   *American football*   **Jackson**   **Tallahassee**

Austin   *Oil*   **Baton Rouge**   *Disney World*

Jazz music   FLORIDA

Houston   *Shrimp*

Cargo ship   *Alligator*   *Tourism*

Oil and natural gas

CONN	Connecticut
DEL	Delaware
MA	Maryland
MASS	Massachusetts
NH	New Hampshire
NJ	New Jersey
PENN	Pennsylvania
RI	Rhode Island
VT	Vermont

HAWAII
Oahu
Honolulu
Pineapples
Surfing
PACIFIC OCEAN   *Hawaii*

0   50   100 miles
0   100   200 km

Polynesian dancer

The state of Hawaii is a group of islands in the middle of the Pacific Ocean. The weather is usually hot and sunny, and people come from all over the world to spend their holidays there.

Team Spirit

This six-year-old boy is taking part in a game of baseball, the national sport of the United States. He has to wear a padded glove so that the hard, fast-moving ball won't hurt his hand.

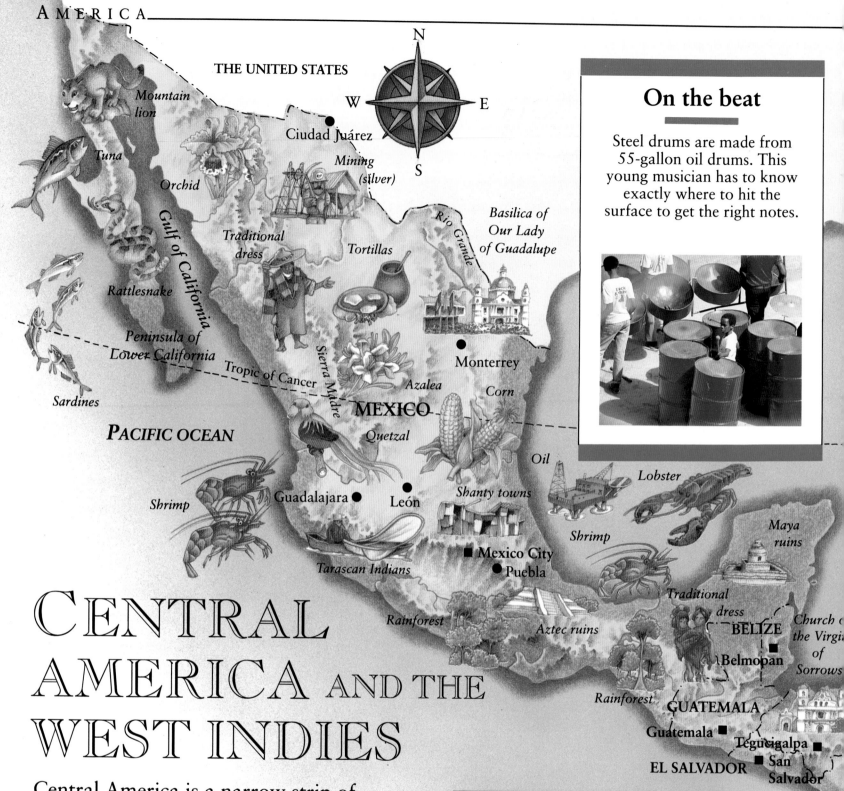

THE UNITED STATES

N
W   E
S

Mountain lion

Tuna

Orchid

Gulf of California

Traditional dress

Rattlesnake

Peninsula of Lower California

Sardines

Tropic of Cancer

PACIFIC OCEAN

Ciudad Juárez

Mining (silver)

Tortillas

Rio Grande

Basilica of Our Lady of Guadalupe

Monterrey

Corn

Azalea

Sierra Madre

MEXICO

Quetzal

Shrimp

Guadalajara

León

Tarascan Indians

Rainforest

Shanty towns

Mexico City

Puebla

Aztec ruins

Oil

Lobster

Shrimp

Maya ruins

Traditional dress

BELIZE

Belmopan

Church of the Virgin of Sorrows

Rainforest

GUATEMALA

Guatemala

Tegucigalpa

EL SALVADOR

San Salvador

Managua

Coffee

On the beat

Steel drums are made from 55-gallon oil drums. This young musician has to know exactly where to hit the surface to get the right notes.

CENTRAL AMERICA AND THE WEST INDIES

Central America is a narrow strip of land which connects North and South America. It is an area which includes lush jungles as well as high mountains and hot deserts. Mexico is the largest country there. The West Indies are a group of islands that form a long curve in the sunny Caribbean Sea.

A jaguar sharpens its needle-like claws ready for the next hunt.

THE UNITED
STATES

Helping on a busy market
stall is hungry work.

F·A·C·T · F·I·N·D·E·R

The PANAMA CANAL is an
important short-cut for ships between
the Atlantic and Pacific oceans. Ships
that want to get from one ocean to
another can take this route instead of
having to sail right around the
bottom of South America. Up to
15,000 ships use the canal each year.
Can you see it on the map?

Mexico City is the LARGEST CITY
in the world, with over 19,000,000
people. This single city has a larger
population than any of the other
countries shown here.

BAHAMAS

Cigars

Coral
reef

Tourism

Tropic of Cancer

ATLANTIC
OCEAN

Havana

CUBA

Fishing

Fishing

Windsurfing

Sugar
cane

DOMINICAN
REPUBLIC

Puerto
Rico (US)

ANTIGUA &
BARBUDA

Lemons

HAITI

Santo Domingo

ST KITTS-
NEVIS

St John's

Cayman
Islands (UK)

Port-au-Prince

Sailing

Guadeloupe (France)

Sword
fish

JAMAICA

Kingston

DOMINICA

Roseau

Water skiing

Martinique (France)

Steel
band

ST LUCIA

Castries

Crab

Kingstown

BARBADOS

Lobster

ST VINCENT &
THE GRENADINES

Bridgetown

HONDURAS

Caribbean Sea

GRENADA

Bananas

Container
ship

Netherlands
Antilles

St George's

NICARAGUA

Port-of-Spain

TRINIDAD
& TOBAGO

Cotton

Panama Canal

Golden
beaches

Lake
Nicaragua

Traditional
dress

VENEZUELA

COSTA RICA

San José

PANAMA

Panama
City

COLOMBIA

Fishing

Monkey

0   200   400 miles

0   200   400   600 km

Parrot

37

SOUTH AMERICA

The continent of South America is over 7,500 km long. It stretches from the hot Equator to the icy seas that surround Antarctica. A huge tropical rainforest grows along and around the mighty Amazon River in the north. It is the largest rainforest in the world, covering about two-fifths of the continent.

Hanging Around

Two-toed sloths live in the Amazonian rainforest. They spend most of their time hanging upside down from the branches of trees. They can even sleep in this position.

N
E
W
S

Equator

Salvador
Maned wolf
Sugar cane
Boa constrictor
Giant toad
Rainforest clearing
Government buildings
Portulaca flower
Jaguar
Brazil nuts
Armadillo
BRAZIL
Amazon
Blue and yellow macaw
Bolivia
Amazon
Spider monkey
Piranha
Amazon
Amazonian
Reed boats
Andean condor
Rubber
Selvas
Inca ruins at Machu Picchu
Lake Titicaca
La Paz
Shrimp
Cayenne
FRENCH GUIANA
Paramaribo
SURINAM
Georgetown
Sugar Cane
GUYANA
Rice
Angel Falls
Amazon rainforest
Manatee
Vampire bat
Oil
Oil
Orinoco
Caracas
VENEZUELA
Llanos
Lake Maracaibo
Bogotá
Mining (emeralds)
Coffee
COLOMBIA
Panpipes
PERU
Lima
Anchovettas
ANDES
Llama
Quito
ECUADOR
Balsa tree
Equator
Highest railway
PANAMA

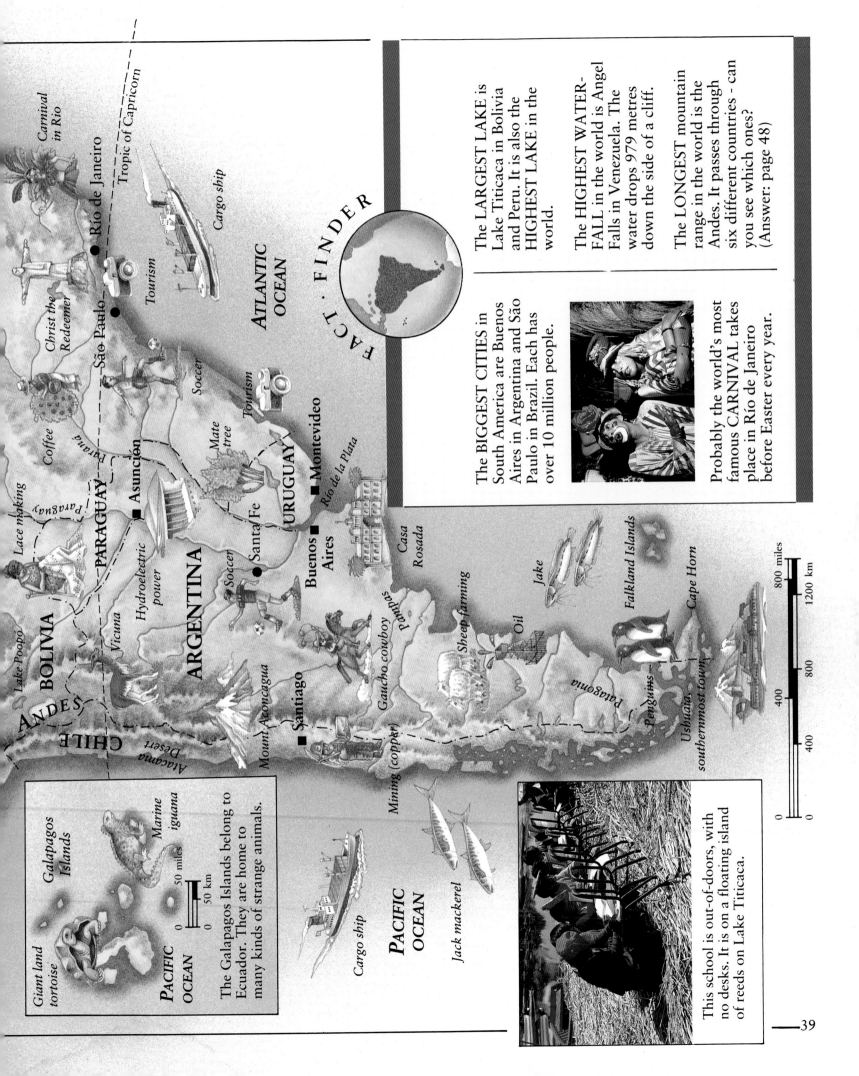

FACT · FINDER

The LARGEST LAKE is Lake Titicaca in Bolivia and Peru. It is also the HIGHEST LAKE in the world.

The HIGHEST WATER-FALL in the world is Angel Falls in Venezuela. The water drops 979 metres down the side of a cliff.

The LONGEST mountain range in the world is the Andes. It passes through six different countries - can you see which ones? (Answer: page 48)

The BIGGEST CITIES in South America are Buenos Aires in Argentina and São Paulo in Brazil. Each has over 10 million people.

Probably the world's most famous CARNIVAL takes place in Río de Janeiro before Easter every year.

This school is out-of-doors, with no desks. It is on a floating island of reeds on Lake Titicaca.

The Galapagos Islands belong to Ecuador. They are home to many kinds of strange animals.

39

AUSTRALIA

The weather in Australia is often hot and dry. The centre of the country is mainly desert, so most people live in towns and cities on the coast. Until about 200 years ago, only Aborigines lived there, but since then, people have come to settle from all over the world.

Aborigine children enjoying the rain after weeks of dry weather.

FACT · FINDER

Australia is both the SMALLEST continent and the LARGEST island in the world.

There are TEN TIMES more sheep than there are people in Australia. Some of the cattle herds are so enormous that the farmers use helicopters to help round them up.

The Aborigines call Ayers Rock *Uluru*. To them, it is a very SACRED PLACE. Many paintings and carvings, some of which are very old indeed, cover the walls of the caves inside it. Can you spot it on the map?

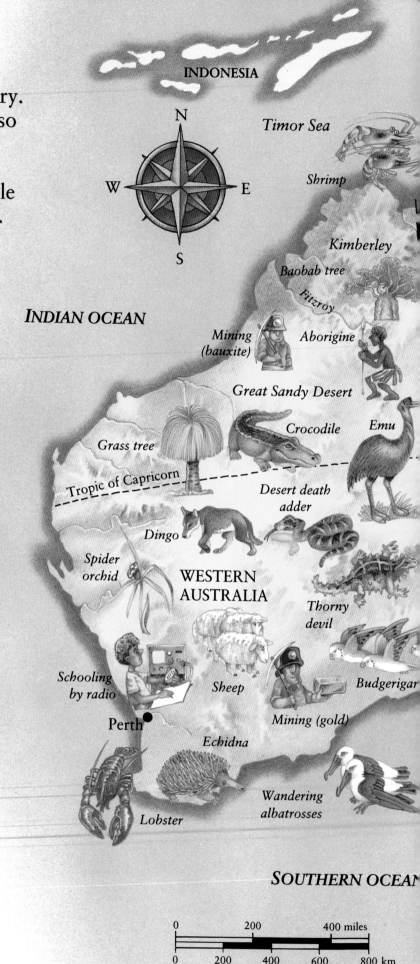

INDONESIA

N
W E
S

Timor Sea

Shrimp

Kimberley

Baobab tree

Fitzroy

INDIAN OCEAN

Mining (bauxite)

Aborigine

Great Sandy Desert

Crocodile

Emu

Grass tree

Tropic of Capricorn

Desert death adder

Dingo

Spider orchid

WESTERN AUSTRALIA

Thorny devil

Schooling by radio

Sheep

Mining (gold)

Budgerigar

Perth

Echidna

Lobster

Wandering albatrosses

SOUTHERN OCEAN

0 200 400 miles
0 200 400 600 800 km

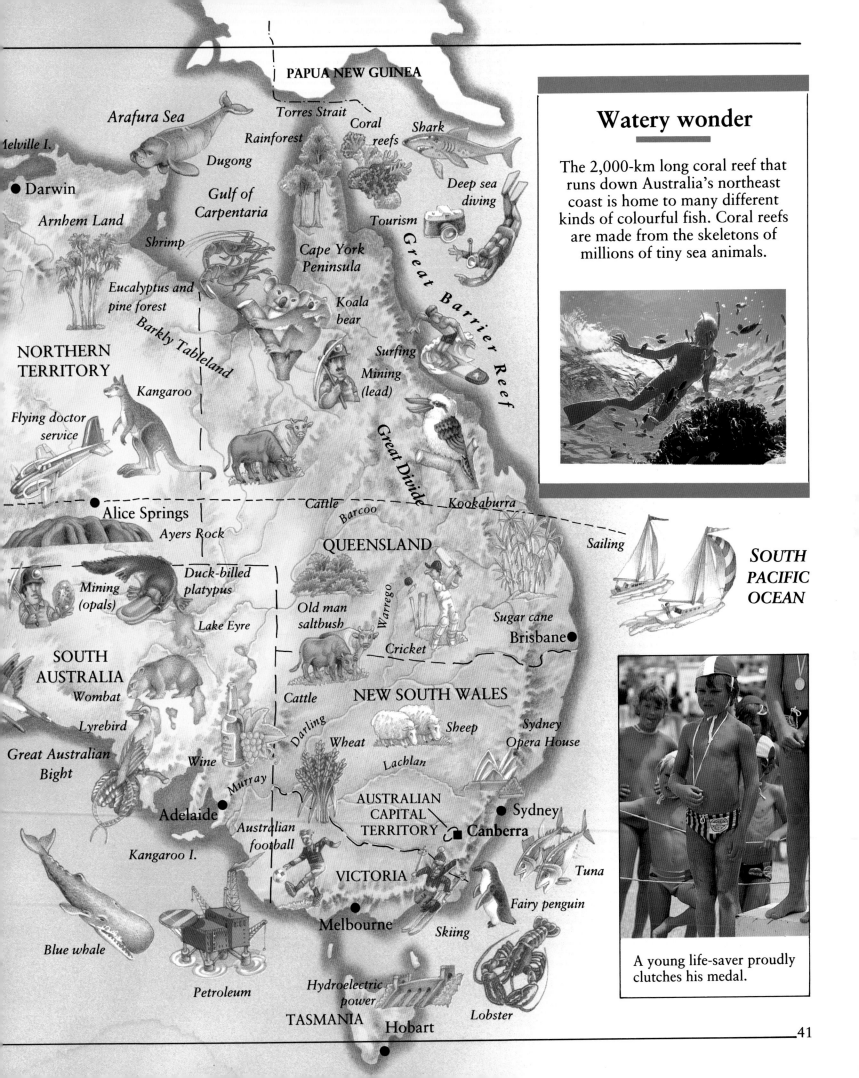

PAPUA NEW GUINEA

Arafura Sea

Melville I.

● Darwin

Arnhem Land

Dugong

Gulf of
Carpentaria

Shrimp

Torres Strait

Rainforest

Coral
reefs

Shark

Deep sea
diving

Tourism

Cape York
Peninsula

Eucalyptus and
pine forest

Barkly Tableland

NORTHERN
TERRITORY

Kangaroo

Flying doctor
service

Koala
bear

Surfing

Mining
(lead)

Great Barrier Reef

Alice Springs

Ayers Rock

Cattle

Barcoo

Kookaburra

Great Divide

Mining
(opals)

Duck-billed
platypus

Lake Eyre

QUEENSLAND

Old man
saltbush

Warrego

Cricket

Sailing

SOUTH
PACIFIC
OCEAN

Sugar cane

Brisbane ●

SOUTH
AUSTRALIA

Wombat

Lyrebird

Great Australian
Bight

Wine

Cattle

Darling

Wheat

NEW SOUTH WALES

Sheep

Lachlan

Sydney
Opera House

Murray

Adelaide ●

Australian
football

AUSTRALIAN
CAPITAL
TERRITORY ■ Canberra

Sydney ●

Kangaroo I.

VICTORIA

Tuna

Blue whale

Melbourne ●

Skiing

Fairy penguin

Petroleum

Hydroelectric
power

TASMANIA

Hobart ●

Lobster

Watery wonder

The 2,000-km long coral reef that
runs down Australia's northeast
coast is home to many different
kinds of colourful fish. Coral reefs
are made from the skeletons of
millions of tiny sea animals.

A young life-saver proudly
clutches his medal.

NEW ZEALAND AND THE PACIFIC

The Pacific Ocean covers nearly half of the world's surface. There are many thousands of islands dotted across its surface. The largest are New Guinea and the two islands of New Zealand. The rest are divided into groups that make up the different countries.

Anyone for cricket?

Cricket is a favourite sport in New Zealand. It was introduced by people from Britain who first settled there 200 years ago.

ASIA

JAPAN

The Marianas Trench

Golden long-nosed butterfly fish

Luxury liner

Coral atolls

Midway I (US)

Golden beac

Aircraft carrier

Northern Mariana Islands (US)
Coral

Guam (US)

MARSHALL ISLANDS

Micronesian islander

Coconuts

THE PHILIPPINES

Fishing with spears

FEDERATED STATES OF MICRONESIA

Koror
BELAU

Palikir

Dalap-Uliga-Darrit

Airplane routes

Bananas

Princess Stephanie bird

Bairiki

Equator

INDONESIA

Tuna

Lychees

Houses on stilts

NAURU

Phosphate

Lobster

PAPUA NEW GUINEA

Tourism

TUVALU

SOLOMON ISLANDS
Honiara

Fongafale

Tokelau Is (NZ)

WESTERN SAMOA

Port Moresby

Pineapple

Wallis and Futuna (Fr)

Apia

FIJI

Forestry

VANUATU
Port-Vila

Volsano

Suva

TONGA

Nuku'alofa

New Caledonia (Fr)

Nouméa

Polynesian islander

AUSTRALIA

Tuna

Coral

Sheep

Kiwi

Auckland

Kiwi fruit

Wellington
NEW ZEALAND

Christchurch

Hooker sealion

Maori

Garfish

Traditional face-painting in
Papua New Guinea.

NORTH AMERICA

The DEEPEST POINT on the
Earth's surface is at the bottom of
the Marianas Trench in the
northwest Pacific Ocean. It is over
11,000 m deep.

There may be more than 30,000
SEPARATE ISLANDS scattered
across the Pacific Ocean.

The TALLEST UNDERWATER
MOUNTAIN is near the Tonga
Trench between Samoa and New
Zealand. It is 8,690 m high,
although its top is still 365 m
below the sea's surface.

Hawaii
(USA)   Tropic of Cancer

Submarine

Coconuts

NORTH PACIFIC
OCEAN

arlequin
sk fish

Clown anemone
fish

Fishing

Monkey business - picking
coconuts can be tricky.

Galapagos Is
(Ecuador)

Equator

SOUTH AMERICA

IRIBATI

Bananas

Tomatoes

Coral

Vanilla

erican
noa (US)

Cook
Islands (NZ)

● Papeete

Waterfalls

Fishing

Container
ship

ue I (Fr)

Tahiti

French Polynesia (Fr)

Pitcairn Is (UK)

Easter I (Chile)

Stone
statues

Tropic of Capricorn

SOUTH
PACIFIC OCEAN

*Traditional
dress*

Dolphin

Oil tanker   *Turtles*

0	500	1000	miles

0	500	1000	1500	2000	km

Sperm whale

43

ANTARCTIC

Antarctica lies at the South Pole, the most southern point on Earth. It is always cold there, and a thick layer of ice covers the land. Few animals and plants can live on Antarctica itself, but the surrounding seas are full of life.

A research ship moves slowly through icy seas.

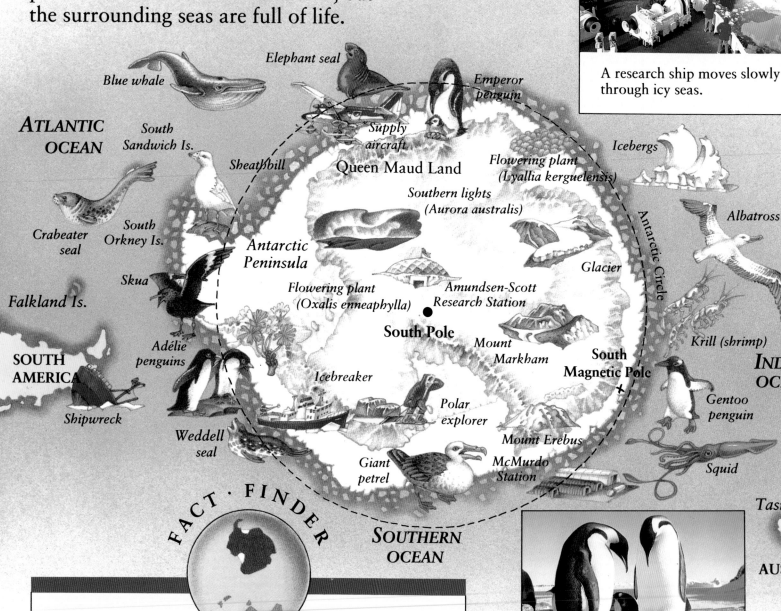

Blue whale

Elephant seal

Emperor penguin

ATLANTIC OCEAN

South Sandwich Is.

Supply aircraft

Sheathbill

Queen Maud Land

Flowering plant (Lyallia kerguelensis)

Icebergs

Southern lights (Aurora australis)

Albatross

South Orkney Is.

Crabeater seal

Antarctic Peninsula

Glacier

Antarctic Circle

Skua

Flowering plant (Oxalis enneaphylla)

Amundsen-Scott Research Station

Falkland Is.

South Pole

Krill (shrimp)

Mount Markham

South Magnetic Pole

INDIAN OCEAN

SOUTH AMERICA

Adélie penguins

Icebreaker

Gentoo penguin

Shipwreck

Polar explorer

Mount Erebus

Weddell seal

McMurdo Station

Squid

Giant petrel

Tasmania

FACT · FINDER

SOUTHERN OCEAN

AUSTRALIA

Antarctica is the COLDEST PLACE on Earth. In 1983, a record low temperature of -128.6°F was recorded by Russian scientists.

The BIGGEST ICEBERG on record, sighted in the South Pacific Ocean, was 335 km long and 97 km wide. This is larger than the country of Belgium.

Sit on Dad's feet - that's a really good way to keep warm.

0   500   1000 miles

0   500   1000   1500   2000 km

ARCTIC

The Arctic is the area around the North Pole, the most northern point on Earth. There is no land there, only a floating island of ice. Like the Antarctic, the Arctic is very cold all year round.

These polar bear cubs have grown almost as big as Mum.

FACT · FINDER

The island of Greenland has the FASTEST-MOVING major glacier (river of ice) in the world. It flows about 24 m each day.

The world's BEST FISHING GROUNDS lie around the Arctic area. The type of fish caught most often is shown on the map. Can you guess which one? (Answer: p.48)

PACIFIC OCEAN

Arctic Circle

Walrus

Arctic fox

Siberia

Container ship

ASIA

Lemmings

Aircraft routes

ARCTIC OCEAN

Evergreen forests

Icebergs

Northern lights (Aurora borealis)

Ermine

Submarine

Arctic Circle

Arctic research station

North Magnetic Pole

North Pole

Krill (shrimp)

Victoria I

Ellesmere I

Polar bear

Svalbard

NORTH AMERICA

Thule

Inuit

Cod

Saxifrage

Narwhal

Hudson Bay

Ptarmigan

GREENLAND (DENMARK)

Evergreen forests

Baffin I

Mining (cryolite)

Fishing

EUROPE

Godthaab

ICELAND

Caribou

Arctic char

Bearded seal

ATLANTIC OCEAN

Right whale

Walrus whiskers

The thick, bristly hairs on this walrus's upper lip are very sensitive to touch. They probably help it to search out the clams that it loves to eat.

Snowmobiles, not dogs, pull today's Inuit sleds.

INDEX

QUIZ ANSWERS

p20   The hottest capital in the world is Riyadh, in Saudi Arabia.

p22   The Ganges river ends on the coast of Bangladesh, and empties into the Bay of Bengal.

p27   The island of Borneo has parts of Indonesia and Malaysia, as well as the whole of Brunei.

p34   The world's busiest airport is Chicago-O'Hare Airport.

p45   The fish caught most often in Arctic waters is the cod.

ACKNOWLEDGEMENTS

The Publisher would like to thank the following for their kind permission to reproduce the photographs in this book:
Bryan and Cherry Alexander Back jacket bottom right, 18, 32 centre and bottom, 45 bottom right; **Ardea/Jean-Paul Ferrero** 8 left; /**François Gohier** 45 top; /**Nick Gordon** 36 bottom; /**C Clem Haagner** 29 left; /**Edwin Mickleburgh** 44 bottom; /**Ron and Valerie Taylor** 41 top; /**Adrian Warren** 7 bottom right, 31 left; **Getty Images** 4, 39 top; /**Don Spiro** 35; **Robert Harding Picture Library/Advertasia** 26; /**Tom Ang** 20 bottom; /**David Beatty** 19; /**Bildagentur Schuster** 13 centre, 16 top left, 44 top; /**Nigel Blythe** 24 right; /**N A Callow** 12; /**Fin Costello** 13 top; /**Rob Cousins** 31 right; /**William Cremin** 36 top; /**Robert Estall** 33; /**Explorer** 14; **Explorer/Tetrel** 28; /**Robert Freck** 37; /**Paul Freestone** 6 bottom; /**Ken Gillham** 9 bottom left, 24 left; /**Robert Harding** 6 centre, 21 top; /**Hart** 16 bottom right; /**G Hellier** 23 top; /**Carol Jopp** 41 bottom; /**R McLeod** 8 bottom right; /**Tim Megarry** 8 top right; /**Bill O'Connor** 1, 30 bottom; /**Photri** 30 centre; /**David Poole** Back jacket top left, 20 centre, 29 right; /**Walter Rawlings** 13 bottom; /**Geoff Renner** 7 top; /**Sybil Sassoon** 22 top and bottom, 43 top left; /**Adina Tovy** 9 bottom right, 34; /**Dr A C Waltham** 6 top; /**Lia White** 43 centre; /**J H C Wilson** 23 bottom; /**Loraine Wilson** 15; /**Adam Woolfit** Back jacket bottom left, 21 bottom, 42; **The Hutchison Library/M MacIntyre** 27 centre; **Impact Photos** 27 top; **Rex Features** Back jacket top right, 40; **South American Pictures/Tony Morrison** 38, 39 bottom.

 **EQUATORIAL GUINEA**

 **ERITREA**

ETHIOPIA

THE GAMBIA

 **GHANA**

GUINEA

 **GUINEA-BISSAU**

IVORY COAST

 **LIBERIA**

LIBYA

 **MALI**

 **MAURITANIA**

 **MOROCCO**

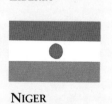 **NIGER**

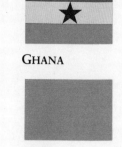 **NIGERIA**

 **SÃO TOMÉ & PRINCIPE**

 **SENEGAL**

 **SIERRA LEONE**

 **SOMALI REPUBLIC**

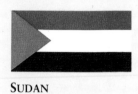 **SUDAN**

 **TOGO**

 **TUNISIA**

 **WESTERN SAHARA**

 **ANGOLA**

BOTSWANA

 **BURUNDI**

 **COMOROS**

 **CONGO**

 **GABON**

 **KENYA**

 **LESOTHO**

 **MADAGASCAR**

 **MALAWI**

 **MAURITIUS**

 MOZAMBIQUE

 NAMIBIA

 **RWANDA**

 **SEYCHELLES**

 **SOUTH AFRICA**

 **SWAZILAND**

 TANZANIA

 **UGANDA**

 **ZAIRE**

ZAMBIA

 **ZIMBABWE**

 **CANADA**

 **UNITED STATES OF AMERICA**

 **ANTIGUA & BARBUDA**

 **BAHAMAS**

 **BARBADOS**

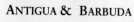